CHASING
MASTERY

CHASING
MASTERY

25 LESSONS

*to Cultivate Your Full Potential
in Endurance Sports*

MATT FITZGERALD

PUBLISHING

 **PUBLISHING**

80/20 Publishing, LLC
1073 Oberland Drive
Midway, UT 84043
www.8020books.com

Distributed in the United States and Canada by Simon & Schuster

Library of Congress Control Number: 2024952158
ISBN 979-8-9907958-0-8 print
ISBN 979-8-9907958-1-5 ebook
Cover and interior design by Vicki Hopewell
Cover photo: Graeme Murray

CONTENTS

PREFACE

When I finished writing this book and sat down to read it from beginning to end, I discovered an elephant in the room. *Chasing Mastery* is about reaching your full potential as an endurance athlete. Few athletes ever truly master their sport in this way, and if you talk to them, they will tell you they couldn't have done it without good coaching.

That's the elephant.

Some athletes are destined for mastery, while others, frankly, just don't have what it takes to fulfill their own potential. That's because most of what it takes to fulfill potential lies within a person. But environment matters, too, and you'd be hard-pressed to find an athlete who got as good as they could possibly be at a sport without being helped by a coach or two along the way. Yet nowhere in the chapters ahead do I explicitly state that you'll probably need a coach if you want to master your sport (though the text does imply it, hence the elephant), so I'm stating it here, in fairness to you.

Long ago my father authored a bestselling fitness manual, the cover of which proclaimed, "Nothing to Buy but This Book!" It was true—the regimen prescribed by Tom Fitzgerald in *Get Tough!* required no equipment, just like the US Navy Special Forces physical conditioning program it was based on. I wanted *Chasing Mastery* to be as self-contained as my dad's book, providing everything an endurance athlete needs to master their sport. The developmental framework offered in these pages serves as a journey to mastery, the individual lessons as turn-by-turn guidance, and, to the extent that one person can coach another in this medium, I'll coach you through the five pillars of athlete development. But a good coach always levels with their athletes, and I'm leveling with you in saying your chances of becoming the very best athlete you can be will be greatly improved if you also work one-on-one with a good coach.

Lucky for me, I know a lot of exceptional coaches. Some are alumni of the Coaches of Color Initiative, an apprenticeship program I started in 2021. Others have completed the 80/20 Endurance coach certification program that I developed with David Warden and Leyla Porteous. Still others work alongside me at Dream Run Club, an online coaching service for runners. If you want my help in matching you up with the right coach, hit me up by email at matt@dreamruncamp.com.

With or without a coach, you will benefit from applying the lessons I've assembled here for you. At the same time, I wouldn't feel comfortable claiming there's "nothing to buy but this book" in your journey toward mastery.

Have you seen that elephant? It was here a minute ago . . .

INTRODUCTION

The Path to Mastery

What does it mean to be good at a sport? If you're like most athletes, it means one thing: performance, objectively quantified and strictly ranked. A 2:30 marathoner is said to be better at running than a 3:30 marathoner, for example, because a 2:30 marathon is faster than a 3:30 marathon. Pretty straightforward.

But suppose the faster runner in this example, who is young and talented, has fulfilled 80 percent of their potential in running a 2:30 marathon, while the slower runner, who is older and less talented, has fulfilled 100 percent of their potential in running a 3:30 marathon. In this case, isn't it the slower runner who's actually better, having achieved their potential, while the faster runner can continue to improve?

As a coach, I don't give a rat's ass how fast my athletes are, because how fast they are depends largely on factors like talent and age that are beyond anyone's control. My job is the same with all athletes— young and old, talented and not-so-talented—and that's to help them find the absolute limit of their ability. In other words, my job is to help athletes *master their sport*.

The word *mastery* comes from the old French *maistrie*, meaning "complete control of something." It can mean other things, too, but the essence of mastery is *control*. As athletes we can't control everything, but in order to reach our full potential, we must control the parts we can—and if we do, then we have met the definition of mastery, performance be damned.

Granted, in the real world, talented young athletes are more likely to reach their full potential, having stronger external incentives (money, recognition) to do whatever it takes to become as good as they can be. In principle, though, there is no reason everyday athletes like us can't find our own mortal limit.

Which is why I wrote this book. *Chasing Mastery* is my answer to the simple question: *What does it take to reach one's full athletic potential?* Among endurance athletes, it is widely assumed that good training is the key to mastery. But if this were true, then every athlete who received quality training instruction would eventually find their limit, and I've known plenty of athletes who came nowhere close to reaching their full potential, despite knowing how to train. Quality instruction may be necessary for sport mastery, but it alone is not sufficient. Remember, mastery is all about control, and if you stop at learning how to train, you will never know your full potential.

The true key to sport mastery, I believe, is not training per se, but *self-regulation*, which is a fancy term for the capacity to control one's emotions, thoughts, and actions in the pursuit of one's goals. Examples of self-regulation are counting to ten to avoid speaking in anger after being provoked by an annoying coworker (that's emotional self-regulation); overcoming a sudden rush of self-doubt upon sitting down for an exam by pausing to reflect on how hard you studied for it (cognitive self-regulation); and putting the chocolate-covered pretzels back in the pantry after shaking out a small handful to reduce the temptation to eat the entire bag (behavioral self-regulation).

Another example of self-regulation is running a marathon. Endurance racing is in fact a supreme test of self-regulatory ability, requiring strenuous efforts to cope with intense discomfort (emotional self-regulation), moment-to-moment tactical decision-making under pressure (cognitive self-regulation), and precise management of speed and effort (behavioral self-regulation) to ensure that every stride contributes to the goal of reaching the finish line as quickly as possible. And it's not just on race day that endurance athletes must self-regulate effectively. To reach their full potential, they must do so throughout the developmental process.

Which isn't easy. Only a tiny fraction of athletes ever arrive at a point where they can look themselves in the mirror and say, "There's nothing more I could possibly do to improve in my sport." That's the bad news, I suppose. The good news is that the rare few individuals who succeed in fulfilling 100 percent of their natural ability come in all shapes and sizes. Some have a lot of physical talent, others not so much. Some got an early start in their sport, others came to it late. But there's one thing these endurance masters all have in common: They are champions of self-regulation!

Consider two athletes, Marcus and Bella, who are exact equals in natural ability and have received quality instruction on the science of endurance performance and custom training plans designed by reputable coaches. But the similarities end there. For Marcus is a poor self-regulator who consistently fails to control his emotions, thoughts, and actions in ways that best serve his ambitions. Bella, on the other hand, is an expert self-regulator who responds effectively to the very same situations Marcus struggles with. Let's take a look.

Diet Changes

Independent of one another, Marcus and Bella each realize that their diet leaves a lot to be desired, and that by refining their eating habits, they stand to improve as an athlete. Marcus, poor fellow, allows a friend to talk him into adopting a ketogenic diet. A big pasta guy, he struggles to adhere to the harsh restrictions the diet imposes, and for several weeks he suffers from extreme fatigue, causing his workouts to tank. He does lose a few pounds, however, and eventually his running returns to its prior level. Asked whether the keto diet worked for him, Marcus answers yes, somehow forgetting that the reason he went on it was to *improve* as an athlete, not to *maintain* his current level of fitness the hard way.

Bella takes a completely different approach to her own diet changes. Understanding that peer influence is a dubious basis for adopting a performance-focused nutrition plan, she chooses instead to study the eating habits of the world's top athletes. This leads her to one of my books, *The Endurance Diet*, which inspires Bella to practice the five core eating habits described in it (such as replacing processed foods with unprocessed versions of the same foods). Because her modified diet isn't radically different from what she considers to be a normal diet, Bella finds this way of eating easy to stick to, and she feels great from day one. Like Marcus, she loses a few pounds, but unlike him, she has more energy—not less—and she performs better in training, recovers faster from hard workouts, and gets injured and sick less often. In her next race, Bella sets a new personal best, beating Marcus by more than a minute.

Pacing Decisions

Marcus and Bella have an important pre-race workout on the calendar—a final sharpening session before a 10K event. Yet despite having equal fitness, the two runners choose different targets for their race-pace intervals. Marcus bases his on a round-number time goal (40 minutes) that he picked not because he believes he's capable of achieving it but because, well, it's a round number. He runs the first interval right on pace, which is good. However, it feels kind of hard—really hard, actually—which is not so good. Already it's beyond obvious that Marcus is in over his head. But he presses on, running the next rep at the same overaggressive pace, gritting his teeth the entire way. During the third interval, unsurprisingly, he cracks, finishing several seconds slower than intended. Having no choice now but to bend to reality, Marcus gears down for the next few intervals, but it's too little, too late. Completely gassed by the eighth and final repetition, he ends up skipping it.

In contrast, Bella's target is based not on round numbers but on a careful assessment of her current fitness level. Having set herself up for success, she bangs out all eight intervals with machinelike consistency, gaining confidence with every lap. Come race day, benefitting not just from this one good decision but from others like it, she will likely beat Marcus handily once again.

Disappointing Workouts

On another day of training, Marcus and Bella both suffer through disappointing tempo runs, each running slower than anticipated and feeling kind of blah. Their reactions to this experience, however, are starkly different. Marcus mopes for the rest of the day and into the next, interpreting his substandard performance as evidence of poor fitness, or, worse, a complete lack of running ability. Doubt seeps in through fresh cracks in his confidence, dampening his faith in the expert-designed training plan that has brought him this far, and he wonders if he should just abandon it.

Marcus will eventually move on from his disappointing tempo run, but it's only a matter of time before he overreacts to another negative experience. And that's a problem. Studies show that emotional volatility—soaring too high when things are going your way and sinking too low when they're not—is associated with poor decision-making and poor performance under pressure. An athlete who broods long and deeply after a bad workout is prone to respond similarly to other challenges and setbacks, resulting in erratic and suboptimal training.

Bella, meanwhile, accepts her disappointing tempo run for what it is: one bad workout. While she does feel a little bummed out initially, she quickly displaces this emotion by reminding herself that bad workouts are a normal part of training, and that it's a runner's best runs, not their worst, that tell the truth about their fitness. Bad runs can happen for any number of reasons, but good runs are never flukes—a runner simply cannot outperform their own physical capabilities by luck or accident. Buoyed by this knowledge, Bella sleeps well that night, stays the course in her training, and, unlike Marcus, brings the same level of confidence to her next workout that she brought to her disappointing tempo run.

Ill-Timed Niggles

In an uncanny coincidence, Marcus and Bella each develop a worrisome niggle in the right knee at a crucial point in their marathon prep. For Marcus, interrupting the flow of training at this juncture is unthinkable, so he forges ahead, with the inevitable result that the pain gets worse and worse until eventually he is forced to stop running altogether and scratch from the marathon. In an alternative scenario, the pain sends Marcus into a panic and he reactively shuts down his training, only to discover that the discomfort is still there when he tries to resume running several days later, as often happens when athletes who are experiencing pain stop moving.

Bella, on the other hand, splits the difference between these extremes. Instead of forging ahead in denial or freaking out and putting her training on pause, she makes sensible adjustments that include shifting some of her runs to the elliptical machine, avoiding hills when she does run (having noticed that climbing causes the greatest discomfort), and modifying her weightlifting routine. Over the next few weeks she gradually steers her way back to normal training, monitoring her body and fine-tuning as she goes. Come race day, the niggle will be gone and Bella will be as fit as she would have been had it never happened.

Feeling Good

Training is going well for Marcus and Bella, both of whom are feeling good as they execute their respective programs. The only problem is that Marcus interprets feeling good as an indication that he's not working hard enough, so he increases his training until he's feeling just so-so, like an ambitious college student taking one class too many, at which point he levels off, assuming he's now training optimally. In fact, though, Marcus was training optimally before, when he was feeling good, and now he's overreaching. He feels so-so because he's never quite able to fully recover from the work he's doing, and he's saddling himself with a chronic burden of unresolved fatigue that compromises both the quality of his training and his body's ability to adapt to it.

Bella, in contrast, rightly interprets feeling good as an indication that her training plan is working, so she sticks with it. As her reward, she enjoys her training and keeps getting fitter, while Marcus stagnates both fitness-wise and motivationally.

———

I could keep going, but I trust I've made my point. Endurance athletes routinely encounter situations that require a response, and in many of these situations, the right response is neither obvious nor automatic, while the wrong response can be costly. Poor self-regulators like Marcus tend to respond in ways that inadvertently limit or even sabotage their progress, while competent self-regulators like Bella respond in ways that advance their interests. Individually, these responses—both positive and negative—may have minimal impact, but eventually they will send two athletes who are in all other respects equal down very different paths in their overall development. Thousands of good decisions and effective responses lead to fulfillment of potential; too many bad decisions and wrong responses leave potential unrealized. And though it pains me to say it, there are a lot more Marcuses than there are Bellas out there.

It's Not About Perfection

Odds are you saw more of yourself in Marcus than you did in Bella in the examples given. To the extent that you are a Marcus, how do you become more of a Bella?

That's another way of framing the question this book seeks to answer. The first step is to switch from a performance-focused notion of improvement, which is all about numbers, to a mastery focus, which is all about control. That's what endurance masters do. You might think the greatest athletes care only about the outcomes of their races, but in reality, they place greater value on *how they execute races*, because that is the part they can control.

Triathlete Dave Scott won the Ironman World Championship six times in the 1980s, but his most satisfying race, according to him, was a fifth-place finish in 1996 at age 42. Although he'd performed better by the numbers when he was younger, Scott felt that he exhibited a higher degree of mastery in his final Ironman, where he moved up 21 places during the marathon following a disastrous bike leg. "No one would introduce me as Dave Scott, six-time Ironman champion, and oh, by the way, he got fifth in 1996," he told me in 2010. "That's a real blight on my résumé. But for mental fortitude and tenacity, it was one of my best races ever, if not *the* best."

To master a sport is to gain maximal control over one's execution of training and competition by gaining maximal control over one's emotions, thoughts, and actions within the athletic context. Dave Scott had no control over his age in the 1996 Ironman. Nor did he control the fact that he just didn't have his best cycling legs that day. But what he could control—his effort, his attitude, his judgment—he did, and the result was a stunning and unprecedented within-race comeback that caused Ironman announcer Mike Reilly to shout himself hoarse when the beloved triathlon legend came thundering down Ali'i Drive, buffeted by the delirious cheers of fans and pumping his fist with a satisfaction that is only ever felt by those who have mastered their sport—and know it.

There is, of course, a strong correlation between mastery and performance. The better an athlete is at self-regulating, the better they perform. But whereas most athletes focus on performance, I focus on mastery, allowing performance to take care of itself—and it *will* take care of itself, increasingly, as the athlete claims greater dominion over how they feel, think, and act during workouts and races.

The process by which athletes transform themselves from Marcuses into Bellas is *athlete development*. For new athletes this process often happens in stages, each defined by what the athlete most needs to continue on their journey toward mastery, faciliatating good decisions consistently and with confidence. Anyone who's just beginning needs motivation above all, for with motivation comes the oomph required to stretch toward personal greatness. Once an athlete has the motivation to begin the journey, learning becomes primary, lining out the tools required to make smart use of their motivation. Then comes understanding, which enables athletes to always choose the right tool for the occasion; individuation, where athletes discover ways to refine and personalize their toolset; and finally, challenge, where the need to stay needy—to never be satisfied—becomes paramount. While an athlete need not wait until every other need is met before they start to challenge themselves, having this foundation for development in place will better equip them to push their perceived limits.

For experienced endurance athletes the process of development is not so linear. The problem of motivation is not simply settled once and for all, and there will always be more to learn. Sports science and technology are ever-evolving, and the same goes for our bodies as we gain experience and adapt to training, the demands of life, and the onward march of aging. Consequently, when athletes have been committed to their sport for many years, complacency can stand in the way of mastery. Every athlete will reach a point in time when they can't race faster or farther—this is why mastery trumps performance. Cultivating your full potential as an athlete with the five pillars of mastery—motivation, learning, understanding, individuation, and challenge—will support a lifelong pursuit of personal greatness.

Let's take a quick tour of the pillars of mastery before we explore them in greater depth in the lessons to come.

Motivation: How You Feel

Any respectable coach of youth sports will tell you that their top priority—after protecting the safety and well-being of the young persons in their care—is nurturing a love for the game. This might sound rather touchy-feely and noncompetitive, but it isn't. Falling in love with a sport is invariably step one in the process that culminates in mastery of that same sport. With passion comes motivation, and motivation is foundational to mastery.

Remember, mastery in endurance sports is synonymous with skillful self-regulation, which we've defined as the ability to control one's emotions, thoughts, and actions in the pursuit of goals. Self-regulation *starts* with goals, and motivation determines how ambitious an athlete is in setting goals, and how hard they work to achieve them. There is simply no such thing as too much motivation in endurance sports, where performance is limited less by biology than by psychology, and by effort tolerance in particular.

"How bad do you want it?" asks the author of a popular book on mental fitness (whose name rhymes with Fat Mitzgerald). Not bad enough to reach your full potential, if you're most athletes. But there are lots of things that athletes and their coaches can do to enhance motivation, and we'll explore them in future lessons.

Learning: What to Do

All the motivation in the world won't take an athlete very far if they don't know how to play the game. The desire to improve is foundational to actual improvement in sport, but no improvement will occur until the athlete learns the ins and outs of training and execution. There are many forms of learning, but the primary form of learning in the early phase of athlete development is taking instruction. Runners learn how to warm up by being instructed to complete a few mobility movements, jog for a few minutes, and do a few form drills. Cyclists learn how to execute interval workouts by being told to pedal at a certain intensity for a certain duration a certain number of times with a certain amount of spinning after each interval. Swimmers learn how to perform a high-elbow pull in the freestyle stroke through a combination of verbal explanation, coach feedback, video analysis, drilling, and use of hand paddles and other tools. And so on.

It goes without saying that the athlete who has no clue how to train properly in the absence of outside instruction is quite far from mastery. Nevertheless, learning affords opportunities to make great strides toward mastery, as there is no law requiring athletes to be passive in their role as instructees. Quite the opposite, in fact. To apply what is learned, an athlete must claim all available agency and engage in the process. Instead of being merely surprised by the inevitable surprises that occur in training, for instance, an athlete can offer feedback that helps their coach with future planning. And from there they can learn to distinguish a plan from its intent and make autonomous decisions during execution to ensure the intent is fulfilled even when this requires departing from the plan. Though the path to mastery is long, it's never too soon for an athlete to start spreading their self-regulatory wings, practicing toward a larger role in guiding the never-ending experiment that is endurance training.

Understanding: Why It Works

When learning moves from principles to practice, understanding takes root. This is where the runner comprehends the why behind their warm-up routine, the cyclist grasps the principles underlying interval-workout design, and the swimmer fathoms the intent and benefits of a high-elbow pull. Understanding is critical to sport mastery because it allows athletes to do more than mindlessly mimic the methods they've been taught. If every athlete were the same, and if the context in which athletes train were simple and predictable, there would be no need for understanding. Athletes would always know exactly what to do in every situation, and it would always work.

The reality, however, is that each athlete is unique and ever-changing, the training context complex and unpredictable, presenting athletes with an endless stream of novel problems that lack an obvious solution. Progress in endurance sports depends on the ability to solve problems as much as it does on the ability to apply learning. In turn, problem-solving requires understanding the deep principles that lie beneath knowledge. To give you an example, a knowledgeable athlete can plan a pre-race taper that conforms to established best practices. But only an athlete who applies their understanding of those concepts can contrive a better alternative if, for whatever reason, the standard taper doesn't work for them.

In a world without crystal balls, the most successful athletes are seldom those with the greatest knowledge, and are more often those who understand their sport well enough to solve problems creatively. Knowledge is mere stuff, understanding a skill. To achieve mastery, athletes must move beyond filling the mind with stuff by strengthening the mind in this vital skill.

In the context of *Chasing Mastery*, my mission is to coach you on all five pillars of endurance mastery so you can revisit and reinforce what you have learned about your sport and identify new opportunies. True to my convictions, I will prioritize understanding above knowledge in the lessons ahead. You might not learn a ton of new facts, but if I do my job well, you will learn how to think more effectively as an athlete.

Individuation: How It Works for You

The real fun begins when athletes reach a point where they are ready to become a true copilot in their development. Some athletes are ready to give suggestions for their own training on day one, overcoming a lack of experience with intelligence, self-awareness, and confidence. But in most cases, athletes need to accumulate a critical mass of experience before they naturally transition to a role in which they operate as a partner to their coach in the planning and troubleshooting processes. Some coaches feel threatened by this transition, fearing a loss of control or outright redundancy, but good coaches welcome it, rightly seeing the athlete's self-assertion as evidence of success in moving the athlete closer to mastery. Speaking for myself, I absolutely love it when the solution to some nagging problem in an athlete's training comes from the athlete and not from me.

Like the other pillars of mastery, this fourth pillar looks different for self-coached athletes than it does for athletes with coaches. Early on in their journey to mastery, self-coached athletes cultivate motivation, learning, and understanding largely by choosing experts and resources to follow. Eventually these athletes begin to assimilate outside guidance in more nuanced ways. For example, they might read *The Science of the Marathon and the Art of Variable Pace Running* by Veronique Billat and say to themselves, "There are some interesting ideas in this book, some of which—including Billat's inventive twists on familiar workout formats—I'll be sure to experiment with in my training, others of which—including her advocacy of low-carb eating—are just plain kooky. I think I'll look elsewhere for nutrition guidance."

Challenge: How to Push Your Limits

There is no end point to the process of mastering a sport. Any athlete who has what it takes to achieve mastery will also have what it takes to continue to learn and grow athletically even after they've approached their full potential. The select group of competitors who get this far don't really *need* a coach, but they're likely to benefit from working with one. For those who make this choice, the coach functions primarily as a challenger—someone who calls BS on the athlete when they're deceiving themselves (as even the greatest athletes sometimes do), who inspires the athlete to be the best version of themself, who plays devil's advocate for the purpose of pushing the athlete to think things through, who provides a different perspective and outside-the-box ideas, and who keeps the athlete from getting complacent or resting on their laurels.

An example from outside of endurance sports is US Olympic rugby player Naya Tapper, who said in a 2020 interview, "I struggled and still struggle pushing myself to the next level if it requires working harder than I have to. I was stuck in this mindset for a while until I worked with my current coach [Rob Cain]. He has always pushed me to reach my full potential and more on the rugby field, and I have been able to use this newfound mindset in everything else I am involved in off the field. Even when my skills were good enough or could take me to incredible places, he was always there presenting me with ways of how I could get better. I am a lot better now with motivating myself to do the extra bits and adding new tools to my toolbox, and I can thank him for that."

It takes a special athlete to know they need to continue to be challenged even after they've proven they're better than everyone else. But again, any athlete who is special enough to become better than everyone else is probably also special enough to want to keep being pushed to even greater heights of mastery.

Performance vs. Potential

I've made it clear that *Chasing Mastery* is not a primer on training for endurance performance. What I neglected to mention was that the book was originally intended to be just that. The idea came from David Warden, my partner in founding 80/20 Endurance, who thought we needed an athlete-focused companion to our company's popular certification course for coaches. But when I sat down to work on it, *this* came out instead. I guess you could say that *Chasing Mastery* is the sports publishing equivalent of André 3000's flute-driven instrumental album *New Blue Sun*, whose opening track is titled "I Swear, I Really Wanted to Make a 'Rap' Album but This Is Literally the Way the Wind Blew Me This Time."

The problem for me is that I've been writing about endurance sports since 1995, and coaching since 2001. At this point in my career, teaching athletes the basics of how to train is a great big case of been there, done that. What's more, I just don't see much of a need for this type of information here in the third decade of the twenty-first century—it's everywhere you look! But a need does exist for a definitive guide on how to reach one's full potential as an endurance athlete. You can search high and low, and you will not find any preexisting resource that directly addresses the question of what it means to reach one's full potential in endurance sports and tells you how it's done. Which is why I deviated from my original agreement with David Warden and wrote *Chasing Mastery*.

Improvement is the great unifier in endurance sports. Athletes differ from one another in all kinds of ways, but everyone who takes their sport seriously seeks to improve. So it's crazy to me that no one ever talks about where improvement ultimately leads. We've all been dancing around blindfolded on the surface of things, jabbering endlessly about methods and measurements and practices and protocols without ever discussing their true purpose, which is to elevate performance until no further improvement is possible. Everyone just assumes that doing the right things adds up to fulfillment of potential, but this is not a valid assumption. As you will discover in the lessons ahead, attaining mastery as an endurance athlete is a top-down, not a bottom-up, phenomenon. An endurance master is *a type of person*—namely, an expert self-regulator—not a sum of good practices. Doing the right things does not turn an athlete into an expert self-regulator. Rather, becoming an expert self-regulator results in an athlete doing the right things.

I'm sure that *Chasing Mastery* won't be the last word on the subject of mastery in endurance sports, nor should you expect it to be a one-and-done read. The real trick is putting the ideas in this book into practice. Its twenty-five lessons are grouped into five sections, each one supporting a particular pillar of mastery, and each lesson approaching athletic development from a different angle. At the end of each lesson, you'll find prompts to help you turn principles into practical action items in the days, weeks, and months ahead. You can read this book cover to cover or start by addressing your most pressing need. Athletic development is indeed a long process, but at every step it rewards those who commit to the path of mastery. However far you choose to take your journey, I promise you won't regret it.

MOTIVATION

How You Feel

Motivation is important in every sport, but in endurance sports it's put to the test. To have any chance of reaching your full potential as an endurance athlete, you must be highly motivated. There is simply no such thing as too much motivation in endurance sports, so it behooves you to work actively to nourish your desire to train and compete.

In this section you will find five lessons to
stoke the motivation that leads to endurance mastery:

1

The more you love your sport,
the further you will go in it.

2

The limit of endurance performance is
perceptual in nature rather than physical, and only the
most motivated athletes ever find their perceptual limit.

3

The best way to know you're in a motivational sweet spot
is if you can describe your current training as "hard fun."

4

Success in endurance sports tends to concentrate
in environments that are conducive to performance.

5

Conquering fear is perhaps the strongest motivation
you can embrace as an endurance athlete.

Love Wins

According to his passport, Haile Gebrselassie was born on April 18, 1973, in Asella, Ethiopia. That would have made him 7 years old when Geb's countryman Mirus Yifter won the 5000-meter and 10,000-meter events at the Moscow Olympics, inspiring many back home, including Geb, to start running. His father discouraged the activity, dismissing it as a waste of time, but Geb enjoyed it more than anything.

Daniel Komen was born three years after Haile Gebrselassie (officially) and a few hundred miles south in Chemorgong, Kenya. He was raised in a hut with 14 siblings, the family surviving by selling potatoes out of a makeshift roadside vegetable stand. As a boy, Komen ran 12 miles a day to and from school. He did not enjoy running the way Geb did, but he was good at it—exceptionally good—and in his late teens he caught the attention of an English talent scout who set him up with an opportunity to compete abroad. His first event was a 10K road race in Canada, which he won in 27:46, establishing a new junior world record for the distance. Over the next three and a half years, Komen set five more world records, one of which (7:20.67 for

3000 meters outdoors) stood until 2024, despite major advances in shoe technology that had already brought down every other distance running record of his era.

Gebrselassie, meanwhile, made his international racing debut in Boston, Massachusetts, where he finished second at the World Junior Cross Country Championships. Later that same year, Geb won the 5000 meters and 10,000 meters at the IAAF World Junior Outdoor Championships in Seoul, South Korea. From there he went on to set an astonishing 27 world records in the span of 16 years and to earn nine Olympic and world championship medals, six of them gold.

By the age of 26, Daniel Komen was washed up. If you look him up on Wikipedia or the World Athletics website, you'll notice that everything stops in 1998, when he ought to have been hitting his peak. Lacking any real passion for running, Komen viewed races as paydays, and as a result he raced way too often during his brief prime. Inevitably, the hectic competitive schedule caught up with him, causing his performance to decline and sapping his motivation to do the work required to be the best.

In 2009, when Gebrselassie was still breaking records, I interviewed Komen's former North American agent, Tom Ratcliffe, for a piece that bluntly asked, "What Ever Happened to Daniel Komen?" In answering this question, Ratcliffe drew an unfavorable comparison between Komen and another former client. "Moses Kiptanui really loved to run, loved to compete," he said of the world's number one ranked steeplechaser from 1991 to 1995. "He wanted to be a great athlete, and he had a long career because of it. But I don't know if Daniel ever had that. He enjoyed winning, he enjoyed the fame, and he enjoyed the financial success, but he didn't love what he was doing."

It is doubtful that any runner has ever loved what he was doing more than Haile Gebrselassie. Dubbed "the happiest man in running" by one journalist, he told another, "I love running, and I will always run for myself." Officially, Geb was 36 when he set his second world record in the marathon, but according to a childhood schoolmate, Hirpasa Lemi, who was born in 1967, Geb was actually 41. And if this is true, then Geb was not 40 but 46 when he won the prestigious 2012 Great Manchester Run 10K, and not 43 but 49 when he told the BBC in a 2015 announcement, "I'm retiring from competitive running, [but] not from running. I cannot stop running. This is my life."

A year later, veteran American track and field writer Larry Eder reached Gebrselassie by phone at home in Addis Ababa and asked if indeed he was still running. "I still do two sessions a day," Geb answered. "I'm telling you: running is addictive. I do my morning session, and in the afternoon, I have to go in the gym. I don't know why—I do enough in the morning—but in the afternoon, my body tells me to go there and sweat again. I ask some other people [who have also retired] and they tell me, 'We don't get it. We don't run.' But for me it's different."

Motivators, Strong and Weak

Psychologists have identified two basic classes of motivators: *extrinsic* and *intrinsic*. Extrinsic motivators, such as money, come from outside a person, while intrinsic motivators, such as enjoyment, come from inside. Elite athletes are motivated both extrinsically and intrinsically, but the highest performers, according to studies, are the most intrinsically motivated. Comparing the career trajectories of Daniel Komen and Haile Gebrselassie drives this point home better than any study ever could. Komen would run through walls for money but lacked intrinsic motivators, so despite possessing off-the-charts physical ability, he came and went in a flash. Geb was just the opposite, motivated above all by the sheer joy he took in training and competing, and the outcome was a performance peak that lasted a quarter of a century.

Most endurance athletes can tell you a story of falling in love with their sport. Endurance training and racing are hard, and for the vast majority of participants, they promise little in the way of extrinsic rewards. You almost have to fall in love with a sport like running to stick with it. And to reach the point of mastering your sport, you must stay in love with it. But it's one thing to understand these truths, and another thing to sustain a Gebrselassie-level passion for sport and the motivation that comes with it. How is it done?

The leading model of motivation in sports is *self-determination theory*, which proposes that athletes are motivated by three fundamental psychological needs that are shared by all humans: autonomy, competence, and relatedness. The more firmly you believe that your present path in sport will satisfy these needs, the more motivated you're likely to be. Understanding these needs and ensuring they're met should be major priorities in tending the motivational dimension of your athletic development.

Let's take a closer look at the key motivators of autonomy, competence, and relatedness.

Autonomy

The reason intrinsic motivators are more potent than extrinsic motivators is choice. Athletes are more sustainably motivated when they want to do what they're doing than when they feel they have to do it. And this isn't just true of athletes. Toddlers say no to everything because autonomy is a fundamental psychological need that we each discover and begin to assert (to the exasperation of our parents) around age 2.

Daniel Komen did not want to run. He needed to run to lift himself and his family out of hunger. And though it's true that nobody forced him to run, running didn't feel like a choice to him. That's why his motivation for training flagged so quickly when success filled his belly and gave him the freedom to do what he really wanted to do: relax.

Haile Gebrselassie did want to run, and unlike Komen, he never felt that he had to run to survive. As a matter of fact, not running would have been a hell of a lot easier for the son of a father who considered running a waste of time. Both Geb and Komen had good reasons to run. But Geb's reason satisfied his need for autonomy, and Komen's did not.

In 2008, French and Canadian researchers surveyed 101 athletes on the eve of a judo tournament. They found that athletes who reported higher levels of autonomy support (or support in making their own decisions) from their coaches also reported higher levels of motivation and performed better in the tournament. Coaches make a lot of decisions for their athletes—that's part of their job—but the best ones are always looking for ways to involve athletes in the decision-making process. Hall of Fame college basketball coach Pat Summit wrote in her memoir, *Summit Up*, "Everything within our system was . . . designed to teach players to make good independent judgments." As an endurance coach, I support my athletes' autonomy in a variety of ways, including sometimes allowing them to choose from among two or more options for their next workout. I'll elaborate on this technique in a future lesson.

Self-coached athletes have more autonomy than athletes with coaches, but this doesn't always mean their need for autonomy is better met. Imagine you're aboard a jumbo jet whose pilot has been incapacitated by a medical event, and your fellow passengers nominate you to land the sucker. Would you rather have the support of an air traffic controller in this situation or be left to figure it out on your own? Similarly, athletes who lack the knowledge and confidence to make all their own decisions tend to feel more autonomous, hence more motivated, when their decision-making process is supported by a coach or mentor who grants them some freedom, but not too much. This is something to think about.

Competence

Among the most powerful intrinsic motivators for athletes is the feeling that they are improving in their sport. Like autonomy, competence is a universal human need, present from birth. The existence of this need explains why children prefer the challenge of mastering new skills (such as riding a two-wheel bike) to the comfort of practicing familiar skills (like riding with training wheels). In sports, this need for competence is compounded by a secondary need to feel that the effort being invested in training is worthwhile. Evidence of improvement supplies this feeling and motivates athletes to give a better effort.

One mustn't get too hung up on this type of validation, however. Athletes whose motivation depends on constant empirical proof of progress tend to hold back from fully committing to their training because they're always waiting on information that will determine whether their investment was justified. Achieving sport mastery requires more of a process focus, where the need for competence is satisfied by aiming for successful execution of training. Athletes with this mindset are able to satisfy their need for competence in an ongoing way, by simply doing the work with intentionality and mindful attention, and they are rewarded with higher levels of sustained motivation.

When I analyze an athlete's workout, I focus more on execution, or how well they fulfilled the intent of the workout, than I do on performance. I'd much rather award an A for execution and a B for performance than the reverse, and my athletes know it. My aim is to cultivate a process orientation in athletes that satisfies their need for competence and keeps them motivated. It's a delicate balance.

Relatedness

Human beings are social animals. As such, we have a fundamental need for interpersonal and group connections, and we draw a large portion of our motivation from social relatedness. This is why endurance athletes view sports participation as meaningful, and why they perform better with others than alone.

Our social nature is also one of the reasons athletes who have a coach they admire, respect, and trust tend to be more motivated than athletes with weaker coach relationships or none at all. This was shown in a 2020 study by Brazilian researchers who found that, within a group of 301 student-athletes, those who perceived themselves as having a strong personal bond with their coach reported higher levels of motivation, the quality of this relationship accounting for between 17 and 21 percent of the variance in motivation levels.

"To be a technically good coach is one thing," wrote Loughborough University psychologist Sophia Jowett in a 2016 paper on relational coaching in sport, "but what gives the coach the 'edge' (i.e., the extra effectiveness) in this unforgiving and relentless competitive sport environment is the connection developed between the coach and athlete. It is this connection that makes a difference to technical coaching because it supplies coaches with the key to opening the door to their athletes' capabilities, capacities, and potential."

Most successful coaches would agree. "Coaching is 90 percent creating an environment and 10 percent strategy" is how NBA coach Steve Kerr put it. While we can quibble about the percentages, the point is that a technically good coach who builds great relationships will get more out of their athletes than a technically great coach who builds good relationships. The more an athlete loves their sport, the better they will perform, and the more they love their coach, the more they'll love their sport. Other sources of motivating relationships for athletes include training partners, clubs, teams, and online groups.

Tending the Flame

Your most important athletic relationship is the one you have with the sport you love. From both an experiential perspective and a performance perspective, it is in your best interest to actively tend the flame of your passion for training and racing, using every means at your disposal to enhance your sense of autonomy, competence, and relatedness. Coaches can assist in this effort, but it's mostly up to you to nurture your love, for it is truly yours. Endurance masters like Haile Gebrselassie see this as a goal unto itself, distinct from but aligned with the goal of reaching their full potential, which is why Geb kept on running long after he made it to the top, and even after he retired. In a very real sense, those who love their sport most win.

FROM PRINCIPLE TO PRACTICE

As an athlete, you must have a strong and unwavering love for your sport in order to reach your full potential. Here are three ideas to turn this principle into practice on the path to mastery:

1/ Do something specific to make your workout more enjoyable. Choose a preferred training venue, recruit a friend to join you, make a special playlist, bring your dog along, test out a new piece of gear, swap out your planned workout for one of your favorites—whatever works best for you. You have a lot of control over the quality of your experience.

2/ Make an ordered list of the things you love most about your sport. For example:

- Stretching myself to achieve big goals
- The feeling of being really fit
- Self-discovery
- Enjoying nature

When your list is complete (and it can be as long as you like), identify the weak link. If the things you love about your sport are essential nutrients, which nutrient are you most deficient in at the moment? Perhaps it's been a while since you really stretched yourself to achieve a big goal, or maybe you've become lazy in your efforts to seek out nature. Now, make a plan to get more of that nutrient in your diet.

3/ Pick a theme or mantra for each competitive season. Even if you're currently in the middle of your buildup to an important race, don't hesitate to start now. Think about what you need to do differently to increase the happiness you derive from your sport. Capture it in a word or phrase that you carry with you as you orbit the sun one more time. A theme of "Raising the Bar" might do the trick if you want to stretch yourself more than you did last season. "Experience Joy" might fit if training and racing have become a grind in recent months.

Die Running

For 26 miles, Recho Kosgei had no equal among the women entered in the 2017 Warsaw Marathon. On a warm spring day in Poland's capital, Kosgei hammered her way to a 3-minute lead on her closest pursuer, an overmatched rookie from Ethiopia. But a marathon is 26.2 miles, not 26, and as they say, it ain't over till it's over. Kosgei began to wobble on the homestretch to the finish line—first a little, then a lot. Then she went down, collapsing within sight of a victory banner held aloft by two expectant race officials. She struggled gamely to rise and continue, but was soon overtaken by her no-longer-overmatched pursuer. When a second competitor passed the foundering Kenyan, medical personnel decided they'd seen enough and carted her away.

This sort of thing happens surprisingly often in marathons. Two years earlier, Kosgei's compatriot Hyvon Ngetich did almost the same thing, face-planting less than 100 yards from the finish line at the Austin Marathon, a race she was leading at the time. Unlike Kosgei, however, Ngetich quickly abandoned her hopeless efforts to regain her feet and proceeded to drag herself toward the line on bloodied knees.

If you need a good cry, watch the video that was captured of Ngetich's agonized crawl to third place. Medics implore the felled runner to take a seat in a wheelchair as she totters forward inch by painful inch, showing little control over her body except for her head, which is cocked like a hypnotic's, her dilated eyes rooted on an unreachably near goal and expressing a need much deeper than mere survival.

"You have to keep going, always," Ngetich told reporters afterward. "You have to die running."

The 2015 Austin Marathon boasted more than 3,000 participants, the 2017 Warsaw Marathon more than 5,000. To the best of my knowledge, only one runner in each of these events collapsed within sight of the finish line: the women's leader. Far from a coincidence, this repeated pattern is typical. If an athlete crumples to the pavement close to the end of a long race—and then attempts to crawl across the finish line—odds are that athlete sits in first place at the time, regardless of gender.

If this seems counterintuitive to you, you're not alone. The leader of a mass-participation footrace is by definition good at running, whereas falling down just shy of completing the full distance seems like something a person who's *not* very good at running would do. Why then is it almost exclusively the best runners who do it?

The answer lies in the nature of human endurance limits. Research has shown that when you put a person on a treadmill or stationary bike and ask them to run or pedal until they can't anymore, they will stop at a point where there is absolutely nothing wrong with them physically—where no identifiable biological limit has been encountered. According to every known measurement, the athlete can continue, yet they *feel* they can't. What this tells us is that the true limit to human endurance is psychological in nature, not physical. The more fatigued an athlete becomes, the more uncomfortable they feel, until eventually they reach a level of discomfort that is intolerable, at which point they disengage from the activity (i.e., quit). In other words, the feeling that they cannot continue is the very reason they can't continue.

Biological limits do exist, of course. In pure tests of speed, athletes encounter these limits directly. Why does a sprinter not run faster in a short race? Because they can't! But in longer races, athletes never reach their true physical breaking point because they always break mentally first.

Well, almost always.

If you're struggling to accept this claim, it's probably because you think that psychological limits are somehow less real than physical limits. But they're not. Consider the psychological limit of pain tolerance. Scientists have ways of inducing pain in a laboratory setting without causing physical harm to the person feeling the pain. In other words, the pain is literally all in their head. Yet every single person exposed to this type of harmless pain withdraws from it when it reaches a certain level of intensity.

The type of pain that endurance athletes experience in competition is different, and in fact it's not pain at all but a distinct perception called *perceived exertion*. Like pain, perceived exertion can only be tolerated in finite amounts. But it's a flexible limit, varying between athletes and even within individual athletes over time. In this respect it's different from hard physical limits like core body temperature. If an athlete's core temperature reaches 104°F, their body will shut down. No amount of willpower can allow them to push through this inflexible biological breaking point. But there's no single threshold of perceived exertion that limits all athletes at all times the way core body temperature does. In particular, perceived effort tolerance fluctuates in response to the athlete's motivational intensity, so that a supremely motivated athlete just might withstand a degree of discomfort that allows them to touch their theoretically untouchable biological limit.

"You have to die running." These are the words of a supremely motivated athlete. To be clear, collapsing within sight of the finish line and thus losing a race you should have won is nothing to be proud of. But it takes a special athlete to err in this manner—an athlete willing to "die running," who for this reason gets closer than other athletes to their absolute physical limit in *every* race, not just the ones they collapse in.

One thing that most people don't understand about champion endurance athletes is that they are not only more gifted than other athletes, but they also *try harder*. In fact, that's half of the reason they're champions! Talent alone does not suffice to place an athlete in the lead of a major marathon at the 26-mile mark. There are lots of talented athletes out there. The ones who rise above their peers to become champions are those who get the most out of their talent by virtue of "wanting it" more. At the highest level, where individual limits are also human limits, endurance racing is essentially a game of chicken, where the winner is the one who doesn't blink. Every once in a while, it's the body of such an athlete that blinks first, and we end up with the bizarre spectacle of an Adidas-sponsored, world-class marathoner crawling across the finish line.

Talent is really nothing more than potential, and potential doesn't win races. Performance does. And it's motivation that turns potential into performance. This is true not just of elite runners like Recho Kosgei and Hyvon Ngetich but of all endurance athletes. An athlete with average talent who has the potential to run, say, a 2-hour half-marathon will not achieve this level of performance without the same willingness to "die running" that Hyvon possessed. You might not want this to be true, but it is. In endurance sports, failure is always—sorry, *almost always*—a choice. If the sprinter doesn't run faster because they *can't move their legs faster, thank you very much*, the marathoner doesn't run faster because they *choose not to*. The cold, hard fact of the matter is that, unless you are as motivated as the most motivated athlete, you will never reach your full potential, whether that's great or small.

Nature or Nurture?

You might be wondering: Are the Hyvon Ngetiches of the world born with a "win or die trying" mindset, or do they acquire it through life experience? The answer, it would seem, is both. Personality assessments of world-class athletes have shown that, as a group, they differ from other people in certain key traits. One is *boldness*, which psychologists define as a willingness to engage in risky behavior. Elite athletes are far bolder than the average person, and science suggests this trait is largely innate—you're either born bold or you're not.

Another trait that stands out—rather unsurprisingly—in character studies of top athletes is *competitiveness*. Unlike boldness, which shows great consistency throughout an individual's lifespan, competitiveness is amplified by certain types of early-life experience. Sons of highly withdrawn fathers, for example, are likely to become hypercompetitive. An example is Sergei Bubka, a legendary Ukrainian pole vaulter and son of a dour, laconic chain-smoker who once recalled of his days as a youth soccer player (in words that echo uncannily those of Hyvon Ngetich), "I would run like crazy because I just had to win. I could really run until I was dead on the sports field because I had to win."

By now you're probably feeling discouraged. You fancy the idea of reaching your full potential as an athlete, but I've told you this is impossible unless you're motivated enough to risk involuntary collapse in races. What's more, I've declared that only those "lucky" enough to have been born with extreme personality traits or endured painful childhoods are capable of mustering this much motivation.

Cheer up! While it's true that the drive to win or die trying often comes from a dark place in those who reach their full athletic potential, it's not always *dark* dark. Research by sport psychologist Mustafa Sarkar and others indicates that the majority of traumatic experiences that top athletes credit for fueling their ascent to greatness occur within the context of sport. There are myriad examples of athletes who were clearly not on a path toward reaching their full potential until a disruptive athletic experience changed their trajectory.

Take Mo Farah. At age 27, the Somalian-born British runner had a solid competitive résumé that included seven European Championships medals. But the brass ring eluded him, his lone Olympic appearance ending with a nonqualifying sixth-place finish in the first round of the 5000 meters. If you look him up on Wikipedia, you'll see that Farah retired with four Olympic and six world championship gold medals, all of them earned after his 28th birthday. What changed?

According to Farah himself, the spark that ignited his late-career hot streak was the time he spent living and training with Craig Mottram, a record-breaking Australian who lacked Farah's raw talent but took the sport far more seriously, inspiring Farah to raise his own game. Around this time, Farah told *BBC Sport's* Isaac Fanin, in reference to Mottram's group, "They sleep, eat, train, and rest. That's all they do. But as an athlete, you have to do all those things. Running with Craig made me feel more positive. If I ever want to be as good as these athletes, I've got to work harder. I don't just want to be British number one; I want to be up there with the best."

In surrounding himself with athletes who did nothing but sleep, eat, train, and rest, Farah learned the difference between strong motivation and supreme motivation, and he chose the latter. As a result of this choice, Mo Farah is now regarded as one of the finest runners in history, a judgment based entirely on performances achieved in the last seven years of his track career.

The lesson here is not that you must eliminate everything but sleep, food, training, and rest from your life to master your sport. You can hold a job and raise a family and still reach your full potential as an athlete. There's nothing about working 40 hours a week or having kids that stops you from "dying running" on race day or from taking maximum advantage of the time you have to train. The only requirement is a supremely high level of motivation that very few athletes even recognize as a possibility, let alone attain. Yet it's never too late to become supremely motivated, as Mo Farah proved. Confronted with the reality that he simply wasn't trying as hard as the competitors he'd been losing to for years, he discovered what a difference it makes if you give your very best to the developmental journey. The same choice is available to you.

I hope this lesson does for you what Craig Mottram did for Mo Farah. Ask yourself, *Am I motivated enough to discover my true limit?* There's no wrong answer. To try as hard as you can to be the best you can be is to walk a hard road—and occasionally crawl it, as bloody-kneed Hyvon Ngetich can attest. Just don't kid yourself. Answer the question honestly, then make your choice. The science is clear: It is *almost* always possible to try harder, and only those who truly try as hard as possible can claim to have mastered their sport and reached their full potential. And if you're not sure what trying as hard as possible looks like, watch that video again.

FROM PRINCIPLE TO PRACTICE

Endurance performance is limited by the mind, not the body, and only the most supremely motivated athletes reach their full potential. Here are three ideas for turning these principles into practice on the path to mastery:

1/ Take some time to reflect on your motivation level. Are you motivated enough to potentially end up crawling across the finish line? If not, do you *want* to be as motivated as the best athletes are? Make a conscious commitment to take a cue from Mo Farah and try harder in the next phase of your athletic journey.

2/ *The Other Talent* is a book I wrote about the mental makeup of great athletes. "Find Your 'Crazy'" (Chapter 8) describes eight different types of life experiences that have been known to light a fire under an athlete, motivating them to try harder than ever before. Find the one you relate most to and harness that emotion. For me, it was regret. How about you?

3/ Take some time to assess whether you've tried harder since you committed to doing so, understanding that only athletes who try as hard as it is humanly possible to try on race day reach their potential, and only those who practice going all in are ready to try as hard as possible when it matters. If you still haven't tried as hard as you want to, diagnose why your commitment hasn't borne fruit. Once you identify what *doesn't* work, you're in a good position to try something else that *will* work in the year ahead. Be creative. What crazy goal can switch you into your version of the "die running" mentality that champions possess?

Hard Fun

Endurance training is hard work. As such, it demands a high level of sustained motivation. For most athletes, the motivation to work hard derives partly from an expectation that the training they're doing will yield results. Hope alone won't motivate a person to keep working hard, however. Athletes want proof that their training is working, not just on race day but throughout the process. So where should they look for this proof?

The obvious answer is measurement—specifically, objective indicators of fitness. If an athlete's VO_2 max, or critical velocity, or lactate threshold, or some other scientifically validated measure of endurance fitness is improving, they know their training program is working. But it's not always easy to obtain reliable measurements of these physiological indicators. Athletes must either rely on formal testing, which can't (or at least shouldn't) be done too often, or else trust the estimates generated by one of the many wearable devices available to them, and there's good reason to doubt a lot of these estimates.

What's more, even to the extent that quantitative indicators of fitness can be reliably measured every day, the numbers don't improve every day. That's not how training works. Like it or not, getting fitter is a relatively slow process, especially for more experienced athletes. Those hungry for proof that their training is working would find little satisfaction in a perfect-information scenario, where a space-age measurement device allowed them to know their precise VO_2 max, lactate threshold, and whatever else at all times. Weeks might pass before this device (like the watched pot that never boils) showed any positive change.

Some athletes, not content to wait for the numbers to change, try to make them change. I call this the *progress trap*. An example of the phenomenon comes from Jessie, a former athlete of mine who trained by heart rate. When we first started working together, Jessie got fitter quickly, and the numbers proved it. It seemed that every time she ran, she was able to go a bit faster at the same target heart rate. But the trend couldn't last forever, and when Jessie began to experience occasional runs in which, perhaps due to lingering fatigue from the harder workouts she was now doing, she actually needed to slow down to keep her heart rate where it was supposed to be, she refused to do so. The all-too-predictable result was that she stopped improving and began to slide backward.

There are two pieces of advice I offer to athletes like Jessie who are caught in the progress trap. One is to relax and trust the process, shifting from the instant-gratification mindset of the average American consumer to the longer view that is universal among endurance masters—a point I'll return to in future lessons. My other piece of advice is to focus less on objective measurements such as pace and heart rate and more on subjective indicators of how things are going. Sensations such as effort and tiredness might seem less scientific than biometrics to our 21st-century minds, yet science itself suggests they are quite reliable. If a 9-minute mile feels easier today than it did a few weeks ago, or if you feel less tired at the end of a 9-mile run than you did a few weeks ago, that's all the proof you need that your training is working.

My favorite subjective measure of training status is one I came up with myself: the Hard Fun Test. If I had to pick one method of determining whether the athletes I coach are making progress, I would gladly pass over all of the aforementioned physiological tests in favor of this qualitative self-assessment. Would you like to try it now?

The Hard Fun Test

On a scale of 1 to 5, how accurate is the phrase "hard fun" in describing your current training experience?

1 / Totally inaccurate
2 / Not very accurate
3 / Somewhat accurate
4 / Very accurate
5 / Perfectly accurate

The correct answer—I mean, the ideal answer—is 5. The harder an athlete's training feels while remaining fun, and the more fun their training seems while remaining hard, the more certain the athlete can be that the process is working. Simply put, your training program must be both hard and fun to be optimally effective, and if it is both hard and fun, no further evidence is needed to show it's working.

Feelings are not arbitrary. When training feels hard, your body is telling you something. And when it's fun, it's fun for reasons that are relevant to the goals of getting fitter and performing better. In our technology-saturated modern existence, we tend to think of feelings as being less dependable or valid than objective measurements, but where endurance training is concerned, the opposite is true.

Just ask Anna Saw, an Australian sports scientist who, along with colleagues Luana Main and Paul Gastin, authored a 2020 review of prior research on objective and subjective measures of training responses in endurance athletes. A total of 56 studies were analyzed, all of which looked at how objective metrics such as salivary cortisol levels and subjective metrics such as mood state related to changes in training load. Saw's team found that in nearly half of the studies, objective and subjective metrics disagreed on how the athlete was responding to the training load, and in 86 percent of these cases, subjective measures more closely tracked actual changes in how hard they were training. They concluded, "Subjective measures, particularly measures of mood disturbance, perceived stress and recovery and symptoms of stress, responded with superior sensitivity and consistency compared to objective measures."

The most fundamental principle of endurance training is the principle of progressive overload, which tells us that athletes must train harder to get fitter. And the surest way to know how hard you're training, according to science, is how hard the training feels. This is why the Hard Fun Test is a more valid indicator of whether an athlete's training is on track than objective fitness measures.

Don't Forget the Fun Part

Correction: The reliability of perceived exertion is *one* reason the Hard Fun Test trumps other ways of determining whether the training process is working. A second reason is that, like perceived exertion, fun (or enjoyment, as our psychologist friends prefer to call it) is also a far more sensitive measure of how things are going than many athletes recognize. When an athlete trains too hard, they enter a state known as *overreaching*, where the body is unable to absorb the work being done. And guess what? Decreased enjoyment of training is proven to be one of the best predictors of overreaching. The moment the process becomes so hard that it's no longer fun, it ceases to benefit the athlete. And when training is not hard enough to be beneficial, that's not fun either.

What you're aiming for as a fun-focused athlete is a Goldilocks zone of perceived training hardness. The work of French exercise physiologist Bertrand Baron makes this point nicely. The term *affective load*, which Baron coined, refers to the emotional stress imposed by training. Research on affective load by Baron and others shows a clear relationship with performance. Specifically, athletes tend to improve the most when the affective load hovers within a sweet spot where they feel challenged but not overwhelmed by their training. Unlike the majority of exercisers, you—and other endurance athletes—actually enjoy challenging yourself in workouts; that's a major reason you chose to become an endurance athlete in the first place. When you don't feel sufficiently challenged by your training, you're likely to become bored and restless. And this is why training must be hard and fun in equal measure.

In my experience, competitive athletes are generally pretty good about making sure their training is hard enough but not too hard. They're less good, however, at making their training as fun as possible at any given level of hardness. I think this is because, like Jessie, they're caught in the progress trap, where they count on objective proof of progress to make training seem fun retroactively when what they ought to do instead is recognize enjoyment itself as proof that training is working, and then go out of their way to make training as fun as possible while ensuring it remains appropriately hard.

A real-world example from outside of endurance sports is bazball, the fun-first approach to cricket that coach Brendon McCullum and captain Ben Stokes instilled when they took over the English National Team. "The aim is just not to stymie talent," McCullum said of his philosophy in a 2023 interview for the *Daily Mail*. "Let it come out.

Create an environment where it's enjoyable, where you want to turn up to work and have a good time and be the best version of yourself. Push the boundaries of what you're capable of achieving as a cricketer and hopefully the results follow." In McCullum's case, the results did follow. England had lost sixteen of their last seventeen test matches before he took over as coach. After switching to bazball, they won nine of their next ten matches.

It's fair to ask how prioritizing fun enhances training effectiveness and improves results. Ben Stokes's view, which is supported by science, is that it allows athletes to perform fearlessly and thereby renders them less prone to choking. "I think just releasing that fear of failure is why we've produced the results," the team captain told *The Guardian* in 2022. "When you take that burden off individuals and the team, you see players excelling and showing more within themselves. No one is worried about getting out. You don't want to get out, but when that fear of failure isn't there, you're not tentative and you make better decisions."

There are lots of proven ways to make training more fun without making it easier, but in my opinion, the specific measures taken to make the training process more enjoyable are less important than simply thinking and talking about having fun in training. When you keep fun at the forefront of your mind, you'll naturally look for ways to augment the fun factor, such that the means take care of themselves. Bazball is a mindset more than it is a set of techniques, and the same fun-first mindset will lead to enjoyment-enhancing choices for you, provided the attitude is genuine.

To be clear, I'm not suggesting that training can or should be maximally fun or equally hard at all times. There are certain periods of training (the early base period, for example) that should not be very hard, and most athletes naturally find certain parts of the process more fun than others. It's easy to account for these realities, however, when applying the Hard Fun Test. Just ask yourself, *Does my training feel as hard as it should at the present stage?* and, *Am I having as much fun as I could be at this point in my training?* When the answer to either question is "no," you have an opportunity to tweak your training to make it hard enough but not too hard, or to make it more fun at any given level of hardness—an opportunity you might not have had if you'd focused exclusively on objective metrics.

To this last point, I would never advise a competitive endurance athlete to completely ignore their heart rate, power output, and other quantitative measures of fitness. These things are quite useful. But they're not the key to endurance mastery, which is all about self-regulation—the near opposite of the data dependency that is so rampant in endurance sports today. Getting the most out of your training requires that you know when it's not yielding optimal results and make smart adjustments quickly when it isn't. Paying attention to your affective load—either through the Hard Fun Test or by some other means—is a more effective way to keep your training on track and, when necessary, get it back on track than any objective measurement. Using the Hard Fun Test takes this responsibility away from technology and places it squarely on the athlete's shoulders. Like it or not, there is no other way to achieve endurance mastery.

FROM PRINCIPLE TO PRACTICE

Athletes make the greatest progress in their developmental journey when their training is hard and fun in equal measure. Here are three ideas for turning this principle into practice on the path toward mastery:

1/ Use the Hard Fun Test. Regardless of the result, think about how your training could be more fun without it being less hard, and harder without it being less fun. Identify one change you can implement immediately to inject more hard fun into the process.

2/ Commit to tracking your enjoyment and subjective training load on a weekly basis using the following chart:

ENJOYMENT

Not fun at all ⟵ ————— Kind of fun ————— ⟶ Really fun

| 1 | 2 | 3 | 4 | 5 | 6 | 7 | 8 | 9 | 10 |

Way too light or heavy for where I am ⟵ A bit too light or heavy for where I am ⟶ Just right for where I am

SUBJECTIVE TRAINING LOAD

Combine your enjoyment and subjective training load scores to generate a composite Hard Fun score for the week. For example, if your enjoyment rating for a given week is 6 and your load rating is also 6, then your Hard Fun score for the week is 12. As the weeks go by, look for trends and patterns. Is your Hard Fun score rising, falling, holding steady, or fluctuating, and what are the apparent causes of these trends and patterns?

3/ Make a plan to optimize both your enjoyment and subjective training load in the year ahead. Identify at least one specific thing you can do differently to ensure your training is hard enough but not too hard and have a blast doing it.

Everything Matters

For 11 years running, Flagstaff High School has won either the girls' or boys' individual or team competition, or some combination thereof, at the Arizona state high school cross-country championships.

Between 2016 and 2022, Flagstaff-based Northern Arizona University won the men's team competition at the NCAA Division 1 Cross Country Championships six times.

In 2023, Flagstaff residents accounted for 27 percent of the top three American finishers at the Boston, Chicago, and New York City marathons.

Why does Flagstaff, a city of fewer than 80,000 souls, produce so many successful runners? For starters, it's a great place to run! Set smack in the middle of a two-million-acre pine forest, Flagstaff is webbed with dirt forest roads and groomed trails that offer endless possibilities for quality training. Then there's the elevation. Life at 7,000 feet puts a healthy strain on the circulatory system, which boosts red blood cell production in response—a boon to runners seeking marginal gains in cardiovascular fitness.

Yet despite these advantages, Flagstaff only recently became the running mecca it's now known as. It all started with Leo "Red" Haberlack, who took over as head coach of the men's cross-country and track and field teams at NAU (then called Arizona State College) in 1964. Through sheer determination, Haberlack lifted the program from club status to dominance in the Mountain West Conference. Then came the 1968 Mexico City Olympics, the first Summer Games held at high elevation, in preparation for which America's top medal prospects in distance-running events (Jim Ryun, Billy Mills, and George Young, among others) trained extensively in Flagstaff, marking the city as a prime destination for elite altitude camps.

By the early 2000s, growing numbers of professional runners, including marquee names like Ryan and Sara Hall, were choosing Flagstaff as their full-time base of operations and not just as a way station on the road to glory. So, too, were top coaches like Ben Rosario, who in 2014 created Northern Arizona Elite, now one of the world's premier professional running teams. Around the same time, coach Mike Smith came to NAU, initiating the school's stranglehold on the NCAA Cross Country Championships. Meanwhile, on the trails, a loose collection of ultrarunners dubbed the Coconino Cowboys achieved mythical status behind the exploits of torchbearer Jim Walmsley, winner of the Western States 100 and Ultra-Trail du Mont-Blanc, among other premier ultras.

Now a Flagstaff resident myself, I have a biased appreciation for the town's specialness as an incubator of excellence in running. Boulder, Colorado, is great, but there the elites keep their distance from the riffraff, while in Flagstaff everybody mingles. The local youth running club, the Mogollon Monsters, is coached by the same Ben Rosario who heads the city's top professional team. Team Run Flagstaff, the city's largest adult running club, is coached by the same Mike Smith who until recently led the country's premier collegiate program. Come for our annual Independence Day 1-mile road race and you might see Jim Walmsley calmly clapping for participants in the kids' division and hear former NAZ Elite member Eric Fernandez telling dad jokes on the PA system while Leadville 100 winner Rob Krar directs traffic. Our Sunday farmer's market is a haven for A-list runners (I saw two-time Olympian Rachel Smith pushing a stroller there not too long ago), who will be more than happy to engage in neighborly conversation as long as you're not weird about it.

When I left California in 2022 to start a year-round fantasy retreat for runners, I could have gone anywhere, and I chose Flagstaff. That says it all, doesn't it? Yet even I will admit that sustained excellence in running is not unique to Flagstaff, but occurs in pockets here and there across the map. Sometimes it's an exceptional coach—a Red Haberlack type—who becomes the epicenter of success. Vin Lananna built a champion running program at Dartmouth College before doing the same at Stanford University, the University of Oregon, and so on, conjuring excellence wherever he went. Other times it's a culture that supplies the conditions for dominance. Norway, a nation of summer cyclists and winter snowshoers, has produced and continues to produce an absurdly large number of champions in endurance sports, including running. Tradition, too, has a way of mass-producing successful runners. Adams State University in Colorado has been an NCCA Division II heavyweight in cross-country since the 1960s, maintaining the same high standard through successions of coaches and athletes and administrators.

Rare is the runner who reaches the top of the sport outside of an environment that is already known for success. Rarer still is the scientist who acknowledges this reality when asked what it takes to be successful. The common understanding of success in endurance sports is athlete-centered, a reductionistic perspective that ascribes outsized importance to talent and training and marginalizes the context in which talent incubates and training occurs. I don't mean to suggest that talent and training don't matter. Everyone knows they do. But in the quest to reach one's full potential as an endurance athlete, *everything matters*, and not everyone knows this, which is an advantage to athletes and coaches who do.

Ecology of Success

One scientist who does appreciate the importance of context is Mabliny Thuany, an exercise physiologist at the University of Porto in Portugal and lead author of a 2023 paper titled "Beyond the Border of the Athlete-Centered Approach: A Model to Understand Runners' Performance." Here's a bit of it:

> The athlete-centered approach is intrinsically related to the mechanical idea that compares the human body with a machine, where each part must be understood separately to provide the answer about the "final product." Notwithstanding the relevance of this approach . . . sports performance cannot be fully understood if the subject–environment relationship is not considered. Furthermore, since the subject–environment relationship operates in an open system, the use of holistic approaches to understand the behavior that emerges from this interaction is necessary.

As an alternative to the reductionistic athlete-centered model of sports performance, Thuany offers a holistic model based on Urie Bronfenbrenner's ecological systems theory. Born in Moscow in 1917, Bronfenbrenner emigrated to the United States with his family at age 6 and later became an academic psychologist, focusing his research on childhood development. His ecological systems theory came about as the culmination of this research, placing the developing child at the center of a circle with concentric rings representing various levels of environmental influence ranging from proximal (family, schoolmates, etc.) to distal (culture, political systems, etc.).

In Thuany's adapted version of this model, athlete performance sits at the center of a similar circle. The innermost ring around the core comprises the "micro-level" of influences on performance, which include biology, morphology, training, family, and coaching. The middle ring, representing the "meso-level," includes financial support, training facilities, and competitive opportunities. The outer ring, or "macro-level," encompasses economic, demographic, political, cultural, and historical influences. The second half of Thuany's paper is devoted to applying this theoretical model to the specific example of East African success in distance running, which is commonly and naively attributed to genetics but is in fact a product of the same kinds of environmental factors (high altitude, a slower lifestyle, high participation numbers, group training, and a self-reinforcing tradition of achievement) that nurture success elsewhere.

There are better examples, however—environments where lasting success occurred despite obvious defects at the center, such as weak talent pools or questionable training practices, highlighting the importance of the less tangible elements of the performance equation. Among them is the example of Ben Penberthy, who coached a group of young runners to great success on England's rugged western coast in the 1980s, churning out numerous champions and a 3:55 miler. Penberthy knew only the rudiments of physiology, and he trained his athletes with unconventional methods that were outdated even then. Runs lasting longer than 45 minutes were dismissed as a waste of time. Slow running was frowned upon, track running forbidden. High-intensity training almost always took the form of uphill sprints on sand dunes. But the best preparation for racing, Penberthy believed, was racing itself, which his runners did often—sometimes twice in one weekend. And when they did race, they often beat runners who trained with more advanced methods.

Their advantage lay elsewhere, you see—in the physical and social context of their unorthodox training. Penberthy's group ran at a desolate beach near the Cornish village of Gwithian. Their coach exuded a quiet charisma that, when combined with the rugged setting, generated a palpable camaraderie among the runners, all of whom wanted to be there, even on the hardest days—*especially* on the hardest days.

It's possible Penberthy's team would have performed better with more advanced training. They performed well enough without it, however, and in doing so they proved that factors outside the athlete's body contribute as much to success as factors beneath the skin.

A second story that teaches the same lesson is one I heard from Tommy Rivers Puzey, a runner-influencer beloved by iFit treadmill users. It happened in 2009, when Tommy's wife, Steph, was accepted into a master's program in conflict studies in La Paz, Costa Rica. Never one to miss an opportunity for adventure, Tommy (who had previously done missionary work in Brazil) took a leave of absence from his undergraduate studies in Hawaii to accompany his bride to Central America, where he immersed himself in the thriving local running scene centered on a 20-mile race to the top of a 12,500-foot mountain. Smelling victory, Tommy spent six months training for the event, only to have his ass handed to him, finishing 45 minutes behind the winner in 24th place.

Fluent in Spanish, Tommy struck up a conversation with one of the top finishers and asked him about his training.

"I don't train," the runner told him.

"What do you mean?" Tommy asked.

"I don't have time to train. I have too much work to do."

"What kind of work?"

"I'm a porter."

"What's a porter?"

"We climb the mountain every night," said the porter. "We carry the gear for the tourists who are going to climb it the next day so it's waiting for them when they make it to the top. Then we run back down."

"We?" Tommy asked.

"All of us," the porter said, gesturing toward some of the other top finishers.

Tommy returned to La Paz determined to become a porter himself. He befriended a few of the local runner-porters and spent the following summer trekking with them by moonlight to the top of the mountain and running back down, abandoning his normal training routine. Shortly before Steph's project ended, Tommy ran a solo time trial up the mountain, retracing the route that had humbled him several months before, reaching the top 30 minutes faster.

"That's when it hit me," Tommy said. "Those porters *were* training. They just didn't think of it as training. Going up and down the mountain was part of their life, something they accepted without questioning or resistance. Even though it was physically demanding, it wasn't emotionally draining. They were at home on the mountain and with each other. They raced well because everything was in sync: their work, their group, their environment, and their lives."

I should mention that I heard this story while running with Tommy on Flagstaff's Urban Trail in the summer of 2017, when I discovered for myself that environment matters as much as biology in nurturing athletic success. The 13 weeks I spent as a "fake pro runner" with the NAZ Elite team were the happiest time of my life. I loved where I was running and who I was running with and what it all meant, and I ran the best race of my life at the end of those 13 weeks, 35 years after I started running competitively.

Everyone knows it's impossible to be a world champion without favorable genes. But not everyone knows it's also impossible to reach your full potential as an endurance athlete without a conducive environment. If you want to master your sport, you will give as much attention to your selection of coach, training partners, and training venues as you do to your actual training. In the quest for mastery, *everything* matters, and as Tommy Rivers Puzey put it, everything must be in sync, from the outside in.

FROM PRINCIPLE TO PRACTICE

Everything matters in the pursuit of endurance mastery, from the details of training to the broadest aspects of your social, natural, and work environments. Here are three ways to apply this lesson on your journey toward mastery:

1/ Spend a little time with Mabliny Thuany's ecological model of athletic performance and consider how it applies to your current situation. Give special attention to the outer rings, then list the specific contextual factors that are helping and hindering your development. For example, you might note that the triathlon club you belong to is helping you by providing camaraderie and healthy competition, whereas the long winters in your area are hindering it.

2/ Choose a specific contextual impediment to your development that you are able and willing to change. Don't hold back from making a major life choice, such as finding a less stressful job that allows you to focus more on your sport and other important pieces of your life. I've had a role in convincing several people to uproot themselves and move to Flagstaff, and none has regretted it.

3/ After a month or two of actively working to improve your context, pause to assess what has and hasn't changed and whether these changes have helped or hindered your progress toward mastery. Reflect on what you've learned in your efforts to get the rings in sync and come up with a better plan for improving your context going forward. Perhaps this is the year you hire a coach or fire the one you've got and get a better one. Remember, *everything* matters!

Fear Not

Sharks and earthquakes are scary. But do you know what else is scary? Fear itself. Psychologists call it phobophobia—fear of fear—and it explains why most of us would rather not talk about our fears, at least not right now. Boo!

Seriously, though, I have strong beliefs about fear as it relates to endurance sports. You might not like all of them, but I encourage you to receive them with an open mind, as I know of no other athlete whose relationship with fear has changed as radically for the better as mine has over the years. If the lessons I learned about fear in the process of bootstrapping my way beyond it prove to be even half as helpful to you as they were to me, they will be very helpful indeed. Without further ado, here they are:

Strong Belief #1: Fear is the enemy.

I have a visceral memory of sitting in advanced algebra class on a Thursday afternoon in the fall of my junior year of high school, sick with fear. I mean this literally. The fear was rooted in my stomach, roiling my recently eaten lunch with such vigor that I tasted bile.

It wasn't algebra that nauseated me, mind you (I was pulling an A- that semester), nor the man teaching it (a bland and forbearing instructor who inspired little fear in even his worst students). What scared me, rather, was that on Saturday I would compete in a cross-country race with my fellow Bobcats of Oyster River High School, and it was going to hurt, and I had a deep aversion to this particular flavor of hurt—an antipathy so intense that, a full 48 hours ahead of the experience, I nearly threw up at my desk.

I wish I could say this was an isolated incident. In fact, it was the beginning of a downward spiral. Having fallen in love with competitive running five years earlier, I left the sport eighteen months later, no longer able to face the pain it administered. My passion for running had made me pretty good at it, but my fear ultimately overwhelmed this passion, and I quit.

It's no exaggeration to say that fear completely ruined my high school running career, not only by sabotaging my performance (all of my best races happened when I was in the tenth grade, more boy than man) but also by stealing my joy. I wish I'd known how common this type of unraveling is—it might have helped. A 2021 study by researchers from India found that, within a group of 110 athletes representing a variety of sports, the lowest performers were those who experienced the most anxiety before competition.

Fear is the enemy. That's the lesson I draw from findings like these, and from my own personal experience. Most athletes think the real enemy is the *object* of their fear, but they're wrong. If it's pain they fear, as I once did, then pain is the enemy, and if pain is the enemy, then avoiding pain is the solution. However, the most successful athletes are those who least fear pain, not those who experience the least pain. If it's failure they fear, then failure is the enemy, and if failure is the enemy, then not risking failure is the solution. But the most successful athletes fail about as often as the rest of us despite superior talent *because they're not afraid to risk failure*. And if it's adversity they fear (injury, bad weather, whatever), then adversity is the enemy, and if adversity is the enemy, then preventing it is the solution. But adversity is intrinsic to sport, and the most successful athletes are those who face it fearlessly, not those who fearfully prevent it.

My lawyers have asked me to assure you I'm not trying to talk you out of taking sensible steps to prevent pain, failure, and adversity from interfering with your development. But if you want to master your sport, you must also accept the inevitability of pain, failure, and adversity in the march toward mastery. Pain is not the enemy—you *need* pain. Same with failure and adversity. *Fear* of these things (and others) is the real enemy.

Strong Belief #2: Fear is a choice.

More than just unhelpful, fear of pain, failure, and adversity is also *unnecessary*. We know this because there are athletes in the world who do not fear these things. And I am one of them.

At the beginning of this chapter I shared an unhappy memory from my days as a high school runner. I'll now share a second memory, similar to the first in that it concerns a moment of pre-race anticipation, but completely different otherwise. I'm now 44 years old and about to compete in my first ultra, the American River 50 Mile Endurance Run in Northern California, and I know it will hurt far more—or at least far longer—than any of the 5K cross-country races I ran as a teenager. Despite this knowledge, I feel calm as I wait for the horn blast, yet also eager, like a young man getting ready for a second date after a magical first date. Incredibly, I now crave the very pain I once feared, not because I've become a masochist but because I've mastered my fear, transforming my greatest weakness into a special advantage. No sane person—including myself—enjoys pain, but you have to be good at dealing with pain to reach your full potential as an endurance athlete, and it's natural to crave what you're good at.

I am living proof that an athlete can go from being bossed by fear to being the boss of fear—and reap the rewards. We've seen already that fear takes the fun out of being an athlete and sabotages performance. It stands to reason, then, that conquering fear would have the opposite effect, and it does. Studies have shown that when anxious athletes are trained in anxiety-reducing techniques such as mindfulness meditation (a topic I'll return to momentarily), they perform better and have more fun.

When athletes choose meditation or some other method of relaxing the mind, they choose to be less afraid, and in exercising this choice they benefit. I certainly did. Out of 525 participants in my first ultra, I beat 511, and although the experience was even more painful than expected, my fearless choice to embrace the pain enabled me to enjoy every second of the seven-plus hours it took me to finish the race.

Strong Belief #3: The best way to conquer fear is to go straight at it.

In the clinical setting, psychologists treat phobias, panic attacks, PTSD, and other fear-based disorders with immersion therapy, which involves graded exposure to the object of fear. Immersion therapy for fear of flying, for example, starts with sitting in a flight simulator. I didn't know the first thing about immersion therapy when I set out to conquer my fear of race pain, but the three-step process that resulted from following my intuition resembles it, and offers a road map to any athlete looking to become less afraid.

STEP 1: NAME YOUR FEAR.

We can't overcome fears we don't acknowledge. But acknowledging our fears isn't easy, especially when doing so pulls the cover off something we'd rather not see about ourselves. As a young runner, I did some downright cowardly things to escape the discomfort of racing, including once faking an ankle injury during a race. It wasn't until I got back into running in my late twenties, however, that I admitted my cowardice and embarked on the long process of becoming the boss of my fear. It seemed a small step at the time, but in taking it, I was already a third of the way toward defeating my inner coward. The journey was far from complete, but I now had momentum on my side.

STEP 2: MAKE OVERCOMING FEAR AN EXPLICIT GOAL.

In athletes, fear most often relates to goals. There is something we want very much to achieve, and we fear both the possibility of failure and the difficulty of success. Try as we might to remain singularly focused on the goal ahead of us, worry tugs at us from all sides, a continuous distraction. The solution I found is to foil fear's efforts to distract me from my goal by looking straight at it, replacing performance goals like winning and hitting certain times with the subjective goal of racing courageously. I judged my performances not by how many people I beat or how fast I went but by how much I suffered and how close I came to "leaving it all out there."

And it worked. Embracing pain as the very point of competing brought me another step closer to becoming the athlete I wanted to be. It wasn't an instant fix, but in taking this second step I gained momentum, making further progress inevitable.

STEP 3: OBSERVE YOUR FEAR.

It is possible—and indeed quite common—to feel fear without thinking about the fear you're feeling. This thoughtless fear state is sometimes referred to as *animal fear* because nonhuman animals (as far as we know) aren't capable of thinking about their fear. But our species is, and when we use this capability, drawing back to observe our emotions, we experience what is known as *metacognitive fear*. In both fear states—animal and metacognitive—we are afraid, yet the two are crucially different.

Metacognitive fear is less absolute. In the animal state, fear is the only thing happening inside our minds, crowding out all other qualia. But with metacognitive fear there is something else happening, which is observation. And with observation comes choice—an expansion of options for responding to fear. For example, you can choose to accept your fear instead of denying it, saying to yourself, in essence, *I'm scared. I don't like it, but it's what I'm feeling, and anyway, it's only fear—I've been here before and I've gotten through it.*

The third and final step in my evolution from quitter to conquerer involved just this kind of reframing. I taught myself to quickly switch from animal fear to metacognitive fear whenever I slipped back into worrying about the pain I'd face in an imminent race. And the better I got at tagging my fear, the less control it had over me. By insisting on looking my fear in the eye, I was telling it, in effect, "I might not be able to stop you from infiltrating my head, but what I can do is ensure there's a blazing hot spotlight on you whenever you do."

Awareness Is Power

Conquering fear is all about awareness. The three steps I just described are not so much active as attentive in nature. Naming your fear makes it more concrete. Setting an explicit goal to overcome your fear makes it a target. And observing your fear places that target at the center of your sights.

We think of awareness as passive—not the sort of thing that'll fix a clogged toilet. But with fear it's different. Its power lies in its ability to make us look away, and when we refuse to do so, we steal its power. That's exactly how immersion therapy works, and mindfulness meditation, too, for that matter. Resisting the natural impulse to look away from fear allows us to name it, and naming it allows us to make a goal of conquering it, and committing to this goal allows us to go ahead and incinerate fear beneath the scorching lens of our unwavering passive observation.

I conquered my fear of racing by doing things that an unafraid person would do—things that were doable for me despite my fear because they required nothing more than mindful attention. Sounds easy, right? It wasn't! My bravest races came 20 and 30 years after my most cowardly races and many subsequent failures.

If a pill could conquer our fears, we'd all take it. But that pill does not yet exist, and in the meantime, most athletes just sort of hope their most self-limiting fears will go away on their own—yet they seldom do. Show me an athlete who is limited by a certain fear today, and I will show you an athlete who is limited by the same fear five years from now unless they take action. Fear is insidious, resisting annihilation by dissuading us from even trying to annihilate it. Not all of us are dissuaded forever, though. Endurance masters are not superhuman athletes who are impervious to fear. They simply belong to that small fraction of athletes who find what it takes to regulate their fear—perhaps through something akin to the three-step process I discovered, perhaps in some other way—and stop it from spoiling their performance and their enjoyment of their sport.

I hope I've persuaded you that my beliefs about fear have merit. Regardless, you might be wondering why I've included this lesson in the motivational pillar of athlete development. The answer is simple: If motivation is the desire to reach one's full athletic potential, fear is the prime destroyer of that motivation—the ultimate demotivator. Sure, fear itself can motivate (just ask the antelope that's trying to outsprint a cheetah), but fleeing fear is the opposite of chasing it, and the most motivated athletes—the endurance masters—are those who are motivated to hunt down and kill their fears.

FROM PRINCIPLE TO PRACTICE

Athletes must use the power of attention to identify, target, and defeat their most self-limiting fears to reach their full potential. Here are three ideas for applying this lesson on your journey toward mastery:

1/ Ask yourself what you're most afraid of as an athlete. When you have the answer, say it out loud. For example, "I'm afraid of sustaining a major injury," or "I'm afraid of being viewed as less-than by other athletes," or "I'm afraid of slowing down as I get older."

2/ Get in the habit of tagging your fear whenever it arises. Observe the specific circumstances in which the fear arises, take note of how it feels, and think about how it affects your thoughts and actions.

3/ Take a moment to assess whether studying your fear has changed your relationship with it. Are you experiencing it less often and less intensely, and has your performance or overall enjoyment of your sport improved as a result? If there's still work to do, make a plan to address your fear more aggressively. This could entail asking your coach for help, hiring a sports psychologist, or implementing an accountability system like the one I used to address my fear of race pain.

LEARNING

What to Do

No athlete masters their sport without receiving quality instruction from coaches and other experts. There's more to this pillar of mastery than being told what to do and doing it, however. Remember, endurance mastery is all about self-regulation, or the ability to control your emotions, thoughts, and actions in the pursuit of your goals. In doing the training you're instructed to do, you will encounter opportunities to make decisions in the moment—opportunities, in other words, to take control of your development. Athletes who follow instruction robotically are unlikely to attain mastery.

In this section you will find five lessons
to guide your learning and implementation:

6

Health comes before fitness.

7

Elite best practices are the most reliable basis for
instruction at all levels of endurance sport.

8

Athletes should only put their trust in coaches and other experts
who are genuinely worthy of trust.

9

Perfect races are only ever achieved by athletes
who habitually aim for perfection in executing workouts.

10

Endurance training is never quite as simple
as making a plan and following it.

LESSON 6

Best Practices

Twenty-one centuries ago, a charismatic Hebrew prophet preached a radical new spin on his people's religion, a message so threatening to the jealous guardians of the faith that they silenced him. But his followers survived, traveling far and wide with the same message, gaining ever more converts to what had become a religion unto itself. Among them was the leader of the most powerful empire on Earth, who declared the new religion the official creed of his domain. In the ensuing centuries, the religion that was started by a lone young prophet spread all over the map, and today it boasts more than 2.4 billion followers.

The brief history of Christianity I just recited is a case of what sociologists call *cultural diffusion* and what you and I might call going viral. Not limited to religion, the phenomenon also plays out in language, the arts, commerce, technology, and, yes, sports. Take running, for example. The annals of competitive distance running are rife with instances of cultural diffusion, where the things diffused were innovative training methods. The same three-step pattern keeps repeating itself:

1 / An enterprising coach or athlete pioneers an unorthodox method.

2 / The method produces superior results at the highest levels of competition.

3 / Word spreads, and before you can say, "Monkey see, monkey do," all the top athletes are practicing the method.

Exhibit A: In the 1930s, Woldemar Gerschler, a German track and field coach, developed the method now known as interval training, where short bursts of fast running are separated by periods of slow running or rest. Among its early adopters was Rudolph Harbig, who set a world record at 800 meters in 1939. Czech runner Emil Zátopek took the method further, using an interval-based regimen to win five medals (four of them gold) in the 1948 and 1952 Olympics, and by the time the next Olympics came around, everyone was doing intervals.

Exhibit B: At the 1960 Summer Games in Rome, the tiny island nation of New Zealand won three medals in middle- and long-distance running events. All three of the runners responsible for these medals were coached by the same man, Arthur Lydiard, who had developed a training system characterized by lots of slow running and modest amounts of interval work. Lydiard became a major celebrity in the wake of the Rome Olympics, and his system quickly swept the planet.

Exhibit C: In the 1970s, American coach Vern Gambetta offered a fresh approach to resistance training that became known as functional strength training. Prior to his influence, most runners did generic strength exercises or eschewed the practice altogether. Today, functional strength training is the standard in elite enclaves around the world.

I'll spare you exhibits D through Z, but I can assure you they're much like exhibits A, B, and C, which is to say they represent a special category of social diffusion known as *contagious diffusion*, where innovations spread laterally across geographical boundaries. This is different from *hierarchical diffusion*, where new methods trickle down from the elite level to the recreational level. Interestingly, most of the social diffusion that has occurred in endurance training since the 1930s has been of the contagious variety and not the hierarchical. Elite athletes have been quick to adopt superior new ways of training, but the typical recreational athlete today trains very differently from the elites. It's as if Gerschler, Lydiard, and Gambetta never existed for those outside the elite bubble. While the pros take full advantage of all that's been learned over the years at the pinnacle of endurance sports, middle-of-the-pack runners avoid intervals or practice them in a rudimentary way, do far too little low-intensity running, and strength train like Venice Beach-era bodybuilders or CrossFitters, or not at all.

Elite best practices aren't hidden. Any athlete who wants to adopt them can easily access the information required to do so. Yet only a small fraction of non-elites take advantage of this information. How come?

We forget that sports are social institutions, and as such they are subject to the same forces that shape cuisine, free markets, and other social systems. In the case of running, these forces function as barriers between the sport's elite and sub-elite strata. One barrier is peer influence. Athletes tend to automatically adopt the practices of their peers, training *like* the people they train *with*. Rarely do 4-hour marathoners run with 2:30 marathoners, so it's not surprising that the two groups train differently.

A second barrier—which happens to be the focus of the next lesson—is the unfortunate reality that recreational runners are more vulnerable to bad coaching and fake expertise than the pros, whose coaches and scientific advisors and physiotherapists and dietitians and sport psychologists are themselves elite in their professions.

Most non-elites also misapprehend what it means to train like a pro, fixating on triple-digit mileage numbers and overlooking the underlying principle of running a lot relative to one's personal limit, which is something anyone can do. At the same time, runners outside the elite bubble tend to overestimate the genetic component of performance, wrongly assuming they're just too different from the Olympians to benefit from emulating their practices. To them, taking training advice from an elite athlete makes about as much sense as taking flying lessons from Superman.

To this last point, science has demonstrated unequivocally that everyday athletes can and do benefit from adopting the training methods used by today's champions. Average Joes and Janes who add pro-style interval workouts to their training get faster; mere-mortal athletes who increase their low-intensity mileage get fitter; and middle-of-the-pack athletes who model their strength training on elite best practices become more efficient and experience fewer injuries.

In 2017, I spent 13 weeks living and training with the HOKA Northern Arizona Elite professional running team. My goal was to show what happens when an everyday athlete goes all in on emulating the pros. I was 46 years old at the time and nine years removed from my fastest marathon. But after three months of shadowing the elites, I beat my moldy old PB by 2 minutes in Chicago. To be honest, I surprised myself with this result, which left me with the odd feeling of having been proven wrong by having been proven even more right than expected in my conviction that all athletes should train like the best athletes.

Tradition, Science, or "I'll Have What He's Having"

Not all coaches base their instruction on elite best practices. Some lean on tradition, coaching the way their own coaches coached. Others let science guide their instruction, believing what's best for their athletes is what the research says is best. The problem with tradition is that it resists progress. "We've always done it this way" might work in fraternities, but it doesn't work with athletes chasing mastery.

Science, meanwhile, is harder to translate to real-world training than many athletes and coaches assume, a truth that the best scientists readily admit. Among them is Andrew Renfree, author of nearly 70 peer-reviewed papers on endurance training, who confessed in a 2023 blog post that "science is limited in its ability to provide all the answers to the question 'how should I train?' . . . People are 'messy' and operate in messy environments. Trying to implement a truly evidence-based program is next to impossible—the best we can do is 'evidence-informed.' There will always be a role for the subjective and the 'art' in coaching."

The pitfalls of both tradition-based and science-based coaching are avoided when coaches base their instruction instead on elite best practices. The important facts are these:

1 / Elite endurance athletes know what they're doing. While it's unlikely that today's pros have fully perfected the art of training for endurance competition, their methods are unquestionably the most effective that currently exist or have ever existed.
2 / Elite endurance athletes are human, and non-elite endurance athletes are also human. The bodies of all human athletes are fundamentally the same.
3 / With proper scaling, the training methods that the most gifted human athletes rely on to reach their full potential can and will enable everyday human athletes to do the same.

Not all athletes get to choose their coach, but if you can, choose one whose instruction is grounded in elite best practices. Better yet, choose a coach who takes their cues from the pros while also making use of tradition and science. As a secondary basis of coaching instruction, tradition has a lot to offer. Ask any great coach how they became great and they will thank a mentor or two. Likewise, a coach who bases their instruction on elite best practices but also pays attention to science is likely to train their athletes with a greater command of the complexities and nuances of the process than a coach who pays no attention to science.

The Other Barrier

Six years after my stint with Northern Arizona Elite, I returned to Flagstaff to build Dream Run Camp, a fantasy retreat for adult runners whose mission is to make available to anyone who wants it the "fake pro runner" experience I'd enjoyed. Dreamer Runners stay for up to 12 weeks in a house filled with athlete-specific amenities ranging from a commercial-quality gym to a hyperbaric chamber, experiencing what it's like to be a real pro runner and seeing for themselves that what works best for top athletes works best for all athletes. It's a small-scale operation, but it has a broader purpose. For every runner who comes to Dream Run Camp and leaves transformed, hundreds more are inspired at a distance by what happens here, internalizing our core message that you don't have to be an Olympian to benefit from doing what Olympians do to reach their full potential.

I'm under no illusion that my efforts to promote hierarchical diffusion of endurance training methods will have the kind of impact that Jesus had with his message. It won't surprise me if 20 years from now the pros are still doing one thing while everyone else is doing something else. The fact of the matter is that, in addition to the barriers I cited earlier, non-elite athletes like us just aren't as committed to our sport as the elites, which is understandable. After all, we hobbyists don't risk losing our very livelihood if we fall short of our potential, whereas the pros have to win if they want to eat. But what bugs me is that many non-elites also feel unworthy of going all the way with the sport they love—believing that they have no business keying off the pros.

I gave myself permission to chase my absolute limit as an endurance athlete despite lacking the talent to make a living at it, and I want you to give yourself the same permission. Every athlete is good enough to find out how good they can be. Perceived lack of talent is not a valid reason to train less efficiently than the genetic lottery winners. If higher priorities keep you from making the same choice I made with the permission I gave myself, that's okay. What's not okay is to disqualify yourself from discovering your absolute limit just because you don't feel deserving of the experience.

The bottom line is this: The only methods that will enable you to reach your full potential are the methods the pros rely on to reach their full potential. No athlete should ever fail to benefit from these methods simply because they were never given the opportunity. Inasmuch as I have the power to do so, I hereby grant you that opportunity. What you do with it is up to you.

FROM PRINCIPLE TO PRACTICE

To become the best athlete you can be, you must model your training after the elites. Here are three ideas for applying this lesson in your journey toward mastery:

1/ Take a step toward learning more about how elite athletes today train for your sport. If you're a runner, this could entail buying a copy of the book *Run Like a Pro (Even If You're Slow)*, which I coauthored with elite coach Ben Rosario; subscribing to the Sweat Elite website; or following individual professionals on Strava.

2/ Make a list of five things that, based on your research, elite athletes do and you currently do not, but could. Examples are doing form drills, getting massages, and undergoing physiological testing. How many of these things are you willing to start doing now? It's okay to start with one, but make sure you start!

3/ Take your education in elite best practices a step further by finding ways to interact directly with elite athletes and coaches. This could entail attending a running camp hosted by pro athletes or coaches, asking questions on their social media feeds, or hiring an elite-level coach who also works with recreational athletes to be *your* coach.

Consider the Source

Trust is fundamental to the learning stage of athletic development. Before you can benefit from instruction, you must first choose instructors, and if you're like most athletes, you prioritize trust when deciding whom to take instruction from. By "instructors," I mean coaches mainly, but it's important that you also trust anyone else you take instruction from, including influencers, fellow athletes, sports psychologists, personal trainers, nutritionists, physiotherapists, physicians, and AI training-plan generators. So when you see the word "coach" in this chapter, think "instructors of all kinds."

According to science, trust is among the most powerful determinants of outcomes in coach-athlete relationships. A 2013 study authored by Zhu Zhang and Packianathan Chelladurai and published in the *Journal of Sport and Health Science* found that, within a group of 215 club-level athletes, those who most trusted their coaches reported higher levels of commitment, willingness to cooperate, and perceived performance. Similar findings have been reported in nonathletic environments. Neuroeconomist Paul Zak studies trust in the corporate setting, and in 2017 he reported in *Harvard Business Review* that "employees in high-trust organizations are more productive, have more energy at work, collaborate better with their colleagues, and stay with their employers longer than people working at low-trust companies. They also suffer less chronic stress and are happier with their lives, and these factors fuel stronger performance."

Athletes are right to prioritize trustworthiness in choosing instructors. All too often, however, we place our trust in coaches who aren't trustworthy. Certain traits are known to inspire trust, despite having no connection with actual trustworthiness. For example, we're more likely to believe a statement made by someone who looks or sounds like us than an identical statement made by someone who looks or sounds different.

People are not stupid, mind you. When we misplace our trust, we wise up eventually. But by then we've often paid a heavy price. Think of all the famous athletes who've come out as victims of psychological abuse perpetrated by their coach. The first one I think of is Kara Goucher, whose accusations against coach Alberto Salazar contributed to his receiving a lifetime ban from the United States Center for SafeSport in 2021.

To be clear, a coach need not perpetrate sexual and emotional misconduct—as Salazar was alleged to have done—to qualify as untrustworthy. They might just be lazy, or mendacious, or self-centered, or any number of other things that negatively impact the development of the athletes they guide. To escape such consequences, athletes need to avoid placing their trust in untrustworthy coaches in the first place. But how?

One option is the "God or Servant" Test, which I came up with myself. Here's how it works: When considering whether to work with a certain coach, ask yourself, *Does this coach want to be perceived as a god or a servant?* If the answer is *god,* find another coach; if it's *servant,* you've found someone you can trust.

Some coaches are all about themselves and want their athletes to see them as godlike, inspiring trust through self-magnification. Other coaches are just the opposite and want their athletes to perceive them as servants, inspiring trust through their sheer commitment to service. Only servant-type coaches are truly trustworthy, although god-type coaches are often trusted initially. The two types are easy enough to distinguish if you know what to look for and what to watch out for. In particular, there are six traits that tend to inspire initial trust in athletes but do not represent actual trustworthiness—unless they are paired with, and exceeded by, six corresponding traits that are only seen in coaches who never break an athlete's trust. Let's take a look at each of these pairs.

Knowledge vs. Curiosity

Knowledge is overrated. To the extent that effective coaching is an exercise in creative problem-solving, knowledge has limited value. It's what a coach *does* with what they know that matters. I'll be the first to admit that knowledge is impressive. In fact, absolute knowledge, or omniscience, is one of the defining characteristics of the God many of us worship. So it's not surprising that god-type coaches who seem to know everything inspire initial trust in a lot of their athletes. Unless their knowledge is matched with curiosity, however, these coaches are not truly trustworthy, and whatever trust they trick athletes into giving them will erode over time.

You might not associate curiosity with great coaching, but if you're around a lot of great coaches, you notice that they're all naturally curious. And science has also noticed. In his book *Applying Educational Psychology in Coaching Athletes,* psychologist and organizational coach Jeffrey Huber writes, "Great coaches are curious seekers of information and are resourceful at discovering answers to questions, finding solutions to problems, and creating novel responses to puzzling situations . . . Curiosity motivates coaches to ask the question *Why?* and look for ways to improve their coaching effectiveness."

Athletes who know what to look for in a coach are drawn to curiosity, which to them signals that the coach has a servant mindset and is always striving to be better. Knowledge without curiosity doesn't impress them. To the contrary, it turns them off, stinking of hubristic complacency. Never trust a coach who thinks they know enough. Put your trust instead in the coach who feels they never know enough.

Confidence vs. Humility

Nothing inspires trust quite like confidence. Heck, that's what the "con" in *con man* stands for! People who specialize in the art of swindling people out of money do so by projecting confidence, knowing this will help them gain their victim's trust.

I don't mean to suggest that genuine self-confidence is untrustworthy. A coach whose confidence is based on an honest recognition of their abilities is more worthy of athletes' trust than a coach who honestly recognizes they suck at coaching. Most of the confidence we see projected by the people around us, however, is nothing more than a cover for insecurity. If a coach acts like they've got something to prove, it's because they have something to prove—to themselves. Genuine confidence is always coupled with humility. Servant-type coaches make no effort to appear confident because they actually *are* confident, allowing athletes to form their own opinions because they know who they are already. You can't trust an insecure coach, for no matter how much confidence they project, they'll bite you the moment you're too honest in expressing how you see them. Trust only those who don't need your respect, as only they are prepared to earn it.

Conviction vs. Intellectual Integrity

Trustworthy coaches are like scientists. They care more about the truth than they do about their current beliefs. Like anyone else, they want their current beliefs to be true, but they aren't afraid to change their minds in the face of contradictory evidence. They also don't mind having their beliefs challenged or questioned by athletes. In short, they possess intellectual integrity.

Untrustworthy coaches are like cult leaders. They care more about being believed than they do about what's actually true. You can tell by the unshakable conviction surrounding their beliefs. They are *absolutely certain* that they are right. Any questioning of their beliefs is regarded as an attack, not just on the beliefs themselves but on the coach personally. To refine or alter what they believe in response to contradictory evidence is unthinkable, an embarrassing inconsistency. And on the rare occasion they do change their mind about something, they deny having ever believed otherwise.

What god-type coaches call *flip-flopping*, servant-type coaches call *learning*. Open-minded, servant-type coaches would rather be right tomorrow than today, knowing that no one is ever right about everything. Don't trust a coach who, stubborn in their convictions, seems to have it all figured out. There's no such thing as a good coach who isn't always striving to be better, and a coach who isn't willing to learn isn't striving to be better.

Ambition vs. Benevolence

All coaches want to succeed. But whose success matters more: their athletes' or their own? Some coaches view athletes as pawns in a selfish quest for personal glory. Nakedly ambitious, these god-type coaches are often trusted initially because athletes see their own desire to succeed mirrored in them. But that trust turns to dust when the athlete fails or messes up and the coach takes it personally. "You made me look bad!" Many coaches have uttered these exact words. No trustworthy coach has ever uttered them.

A hallmark trait of servant-type coaches is what sports psychologists call *benevolence* and regular psychologists call *motivational displacement*: putting the needs and interests of another person ahead of one's own. Coaches who want athletes to succeed for their own sake are more worthy of trust than those who want all the credit. This was shown in a 2022 study by Sorenya Miller of Southern Illinois University, who reported that "athletes perceive care when coaches provide tangible and non-tangible support, communicate effectively, and are committed to the development of the athlete," adding that "from this perceived care, athletes are inclined to perform better and develop a better coach-athlete relationship."

It's not wrong for coaches to have their own definition of success that transcends their relationship with any single athlete. Nor is it wrong for coaches to be highly ambitious in pursuit of success. But trustworthy coaches always want one thing more than their own success, and are quicker to accept blame for an athlete's failure than to take credit for an athlete's success.

Control vs. Supportiveness

In an earlier lesson we saw that athletes are more motivated and perform better when their coaches allow them to be autonomous. These same coaches are also more trusted by their athletes. The best way to gain the trust of another person—both inside and outside the sporting arena—is to show trust, which is precisely what coaches do when they allow athletes to have a say in their developmental journey.

God-type coaches try to control their athletes, showing a lack of trust in them that is itself untrustworthy. Nevertheless, they are commonly trusted in the beginning by athletes who don't know what to look for. After all, being told what to do can be reassuring, especially for athletes who lack confidence in making their own decisions. Wouldn't it be nice if your coach could make every decision for you, swiftly and infallibly? But coaches aren't gods, and even if they were, you could never truly master your sport without trusting your own decision-making ability, and there's no better person to help you gain self-trust than a coach who trusts you enough not to control you. Being told what to do is largely appropriate to the learning stage of athletic development when you are just starting out. But the less you need to be told what to do, the closer you are to mastering your sport, and a truly trustworthy coach doesn't need to be needed by their athletes. They just need to be useful.

Charisma vs. Empathy

Strong coaches very often have strong personalities, leveraging the "guru factor" to inspire and motivate athletes. Not all charismatic coaches are trustworthy, however, and not all coaches with milder personalities are unsuccessful at motivating and inspiring athletes. My friend Jake Tuber, who coaches both runners and corporate executives, taught me that trustworthy coaches are always more *interested* than *interesting*, wanting the athlete to be the focus of attention and not themselves. In sports psychology, the term *engrossment* is applied to this athlete-centered orientation, connoting deep and genuine interest in a person.

Although charismatic coaches are often able to elicit early trust, casting a psychodynamic spell on athletes, the spell breaks quickly if the coach's larger-than-life personality is not overshadowed by their genuine interest in the individual athlete, and nothing expresses interest like empathy, or the desire to understand what it's like to be another person. Psychologist Peter Sear has demonstrated that empathetic, servant-type coaches are ultimately more trusted than god-type coaches who want all eyes on them. In his book *Empathetic*

Leadership: Lessons from Elite Sport, Sear shares key findings from his observations of elite coaches in nine different sports all over the world, concluding, "Success as a leader depends on your knowledge and understanding of people, their emotions, perspectives, and intentions, as well as the relationships you have with them. It is in these vital areas that empathy will give you an advantage."

The lesson for you is this: Choose coaches who, no matter how interest*ing*, are always more interest*ed*.

A Shared Responsibility

Athletes need high-quality instruction to have any chance of mastering their sport, but instruction goes only as far as the athlete's trust allows. Instructors therefore have a responsibility to be trustworthy. But athletes are equally responsible for knowing whom they can really trust—which wouldn't be a problem if athletes always recognized the difference between trust-inspiring and trustworthy. Knowledge, confidence, conviction, ambition, control, and charisma may inspire initial trust in athletes, but the essential coaching qualities are curiosity, humility, intellectual integrity, benevolence, supportiveness, and empathy.

FROM PRINCIPLE TO PRACTICE

Trust is fundamental to the learning stage of athletic development, and the most trustworthy instructors are characterized by curiosity, humility, intellectual integrity, benevolence, supportiveness, and empathy. Here are some ideas on how to enhance the trust factor in your instructional relationships:

1/ Apply the God or Servant Test to your past and current instructors, including but not limited to coaches. Consider how worthy of trust each of them was or is and whether the benefits you got from their instruction were limited in any way by lack of trust. Use these reflections to develop an ideal instructor profile for yourself.

2/ Make a specific choice about where you get instruction that is informed by your newfound appreciation for the difference between trustworthy and trust-inspiring. For example, you might choose to stop getting your strength-training instruction from Peloton instructors and start getting it from an in-person coach you hire after interviewing a handful of candidates and listening for cues to their level of curiosity, humility, intellectual integrity, benevolence, supportiveness, and empathy. Or you might sit down with your current coach and have a frank discussion about how to strengthen the trust factor in your relationship. No choice is too big or too small, as long as it is made in the spirit of trust.

3/ Make a plan to take a more active role in your own instruction. This might entail modifying an off-the-shelf training plan to suit your own needs, or having another frank conversation with your current coach, this time about ways you can help them coach you, or something else altogether. This is the year to build self-trust by validating your instructor's trust in you.

Plan in Pencil

Some years ago, I complained to my financial advisor about how difficult it was for me to plan a budget given the unpredictable nature of my income. Considering that it was Gene's job to help clients plan their budgets, I expected him to push back against my grumbling, but he surprised me.

"We had a saying in the Marines," he said. "A plan is a point from which to deviate."

I laughed. Gene did not.

"We're trained to understand the commander's intent," he elaborated. "So, if the commander's intent is to deny the enemy a key terrain feature, we develop a plan to do that. But if, in the course of executing that plan, it becomes infeasible because of bad weather, enemy movement, any number of things, you abandon the plan. But the point is to deny the enemy the key terrain. That's the mission, and you adapt to the new reality and execute a new plan to deny the enemy the key terrain. The mission isn't the plan."

The mission isn't the plan.

Never before had I heard these five words strung together, but they made immediate sense to me because they perfectly encapsulate how I approach endurance training. The way I see it, a coach who can't plan, can't coach. But even the best training plan is little more than a bunch of educated guesses. Who the hell knows what Athlete X ought to do 12 Wednesdays from now? The future is inherently unpredictable. Even in the absence of disruptive events such as injury, illness, and insomnia, it is impossible to precisely predict how an athlete will respond to their training. Day-to-day fluctuations in heart rate variability, liver and muscle glycogen stores, maximal muscle contractile force, hormonal status, mood state, and countless other physiological and psychological variables foil any attempt to forecast in detail what will most benefit a particular athlete training-wise in the future. Athlete X might wake up one morning with an especially challenging workout on their schedule, only to discover that they still feel tired and sore from their last big workout. What then? I know what Gene would say: Time to deviate!

Effective coaches plan like Marines. They do the best they can to create plans that fit their athletes' future needs, but they do so with full awareness that adjustments will be required—most often small adjustments, such as replacing a hard workout with an easy one to accommodate an athlete's tiredness, but occasionally big adjustments, like reconfiguring an entire phase of training to prioritize a particular component of fitness that's coming along slower than expected. Athletes who work with coaches who are adept at making such adjustments are fortunate. For the most part, they can simply follow instructions in soldierly fashion and trust their coach to make sure they do the workout they need every day, regardless of circumstances.

I repeat: *For the most part.* The one big caveat is that there's a natural lag between the moment an athlete discovers the need to deviate from the plan and the coach's first opportunity to intervene on the athlete's behalf. In these moments, the athlete must take the initiative, either adjusting or perhaps even abandoning the plan in order to fulfill its overall intent.

Suppose your training plan calls for you to do a workout featuring 5-minute intervals performed at critical velocity, which is the highest intensity an athlete can sustain for about 30 minutes, which for you, let's say, equals 7:05 per mile on a good day. But on this particular day you happen to feel mentally fatigued from job-related stress and lack your usual pep. Or your pep is fine but the weather is atrocious—86 degrees with 84 percent humidity. Or the weather's fine but you're just getting over a sinus infection and not yet back to full strength.

In each of these situations, it would be unwise for you to complete the workout precisely as it was written because doing so would defy its intent. An adjustment is required, but to make the right adjustment, you need to understand the intent of the workout. In the example given, the intent is not to run 7:05 per mile in 5-minute chunks *no matter what*. That would be foolish. The true intent, rather, is to spend time at critical velocity, which fluctuates from day to day, just like everything else. The way to fulfill the intent of the workout, then, is to complete 5-minute intervals at a power output you could sustain for 30 minutes *on that particular day*, all things considered. If this pace turns out to be slower than 7:05 per mile due to mental fatigue or brutal weather or a lingering sinus infection, so be it.

Now comes the tricky part: determining precisely how much slower to go. Real-time physiological measurements such as heart rate data can be helpful in these situations. If you know the heart rate that corresponds to your critical velocity, you might be able to key off this number instead of pace when you're having an off day. Whether this works depends on the specific cause of your underperformance. Some factors, such as low energy availability (i.e., not eating enough), reduce the speed an athlete can sustain for 30 minutes without affecting the heart rate associated with critical velocity, allowing athletes to make appropriate adjustments by switching from pace to heart rate as their primary intensity guide. Other factors, such as fatigue in the autonomic nervous system, reduce both critical velocity and the heart rate associated with critical velocity, leaving the athlete with only one option, which is to go by feel.

In a previous lesson we saw that endurance performance is limited not by physiology, which merely constrains performance, but by effort tolerance. The limit, in other words, is more of a feeling than a thing, which means that athletes must go by feel to find their limit. This is why bike racers perform equally well in laboratory time trials whether they are given accurate or inaccurate data during them. They perform the same because they feel the same, numbers be damned. Limits are measurable, but the limiter is not.

Your goal in a time trial, of course, is to go as fast as possible. Succeeding in this aim requires that you know how you *should be* feeling at various points along the way. You might have a certain pace or power in mind when you start, but the inherent unpredictability of endurance performance makes it unlikely that your target number will align perfectly with your actual limit on that day. You must treat that target number as provisional, therefore, allowing perception of effort to have the final say in determining how hard you push. In workouts, of course, your goal is not to find your limit but to give your body an appropriate stimulus, but the same approach can be used to ensure you achieve this goal in workouts occurring on days when, for whatever reason, you don't have your best legs.

Returning to the previous example, if you know from experience what critical velocity feels like on a good day, when the associated pace is 7:05 per mile, you can use this knowledge to feel your way to a pace you could sustain for about 30 minutes on a not-so-good day, when mental fatigue or brutal weather or a sinus infection is slowing you down. Perhaps 7:09 per mile seems about right, or 7:11, or 7:13. It doesn't matter. Remember, the plan is not the mission.

Calibrating Your Perceptions

Unless you're already an endurance master, you may lack confidence in your ability to execute on-the-fly adjustments like the one I just described. You know when the target number feels too hard or too easy, yet you trust your watch way more than you trust yourself, so releasing the target and going by feel seems kind of scary, like letting go of a piece of driftwood and attempting to swim to shore when the seas are frothing and you carry the burdensome memory of failing Water Safety at summer camp a thousand years ago. Be that as it may, you can use your trust in numbers to calibrate your perceptions and cultivate the self-trust you need to make appropriate adjustments on the fly. Every workout you do, whether good or bad, affords you an opportunity to advance this calibration process. Whether you're keying off pace, heart rate, power, or any other objective metric to regulate your output, pay close attention to how you're feeling. In doing so, you'll develop a better sense of not just what critical velocity and 7:05 pace feel like but also what lactate threshold, 8:23 pace, maximal aerobic speed, 207 watts, and other intensities and outputs feel like.

This process can be accelerated in a couple of ways. One is to challenge your ability to find a precise work rate by feel—for example, by guessing your mile splits before confirming them or aiming to complete each interval in a set of eight or ten intervals in precisely the same time, right down to the tenth of a second. An athlete who is able to achieve a high degree of accuracy in such tasks is an athlete who is also able to fulfill the intent of a workout despite needing to depart from the plan due to unforeseen circumstances.

Note that slowing down is just one of many different ways a workout might be modified on a given day to preserve its intent. Other options include reducing the number or duration of intervals, lengthening between-interval recoveries or replacing active recoveries with passive recoveries, and changing the workout venue (e.g., moving from the track to the treadmill to escape the heat). The better you understand the intent of the workout, the likelier it is you'll make the appropriate adjustment.

Three main factors define the intent of a given training session. The one we've focused on is target pace or intensity, which you may need to adjust on the fly based on how the target feels on a given day. A second factor is the overall challenge level of the workout. Some workouts are intended to be easy, others moderately challenging, and still others highly challenging. It's important to know how challenging a workout is supposed to be so you can adjust it as necessary to ensure it is no more and no less challenging than intended. For example, a runner who understands that the intent of a planned 20-mile run is to leave them highly fatigued but not exhausted at the end might choose to stop after 15 miles on a day when their body isn't cooperating and fatigue accumulates quicker than anticipated.

The third dimension of workout intent is context. Athletes need to understand how each workout fits into the overall plan for a period of training to make the right adjustments on unlucky days. Say you're feeling a bit flat but otherwise okay on a Tueday when a challenging tempo workout is scheduled. Should you go through with it or punt? It depends. If you have a harder and more important interval workout on Thursday, it's best to get today's workout done today so you're well recovered for Thursday's session. But if you can push today's workout back a day without gumming up the rest of the week, go ahead and do that.

My goal here is not to provide an exhaustive playbook to draw from when faced with the need to adjust a planned workout but to drive home the point that you should never blindly follow training and workout instructions without deviation. Even if you're a rank beginner who is nowhere near ready to plan your own training, you must be prepared to pivot by your own initiative when necessary. Inevitably, you will make some bad calls, zigging when you should have zagged. But these errors are never fatal, and what's more, they stimulate learning, thereby moving you closer to mastery, whereas the athlete who forces Plan A no matter what is likely to pay a heavy price for so doing (picture someone trying to complete a workout in a state of anaphylactic shock after being stung by a bee!) while also limiting the self-regulatory growth upon which mastery depends.

Whether you're well along on the path to mastery or just beginning, remind yourself often of the wise words that Gene-the-Marine-turned-financial-planner spoke to me a few years back: *The mission is not the plan.*

FROM PRINCIPLE TO PRACTICE

In order to make the most of each training session, you need to be prepared to depart from the plan in response to contingencies such as fatigue and foul weather. Here are three ways to apply this lesson in the days, weeks, and months ahead:

1/ Before your next workout, identify its intent as distinct from its design. For example, you might decide that the intent of a set of 1-minute hill sprints is to run about 90 percent as hard as you could for as many reps as you can minus one. When you do the workout, modify the design as necessary to ensure the intent is met.

2/ Rate the expected challenge level of each workout on your training calendar using a 5- or 10-point scale, where 1 equals very easy and 5 or 10 equals very hard. Afterward, rate the actual challenge level in your training log. See what effect this self-monitoring practice has on your execution.

3/ While exercising at different outputs and intensities, take a mental inventory of your internal perceptions, imprinting how it feels to be working precisely this hard, and not a mite harder or less hard. For me, steady-state intensity, which I could sustain for two hours if I had to, feels like clicking the dial one notch to the right of the upper limit of easy. Silly as it sounds, thinking about it this way enables me to find the Goldilocks zone in steady-state workouts. And if I can do it, so can you.

Deliberate Practice

M astery is about precision. Masterful writers find words that precisely convey an image, thought, or feeling. Masterful software programmers find the most efficient route to the functional outcome they seek. And masterful endurance athletes are able to find the precise limit of their potential in races. But who actually fulfills precisely 100 percent of their potential when it matters most? Only those who take precision seriously in practice.

Commanding the Target

On a crisp autumn morning in 2008, professional runner Josh Cox capped his preparations for the California International Marathon with a race-specific training run in Mammoth Lakes, California. The sun had just risen when a video crew consisting of myself and three colleagues showed up at Cox's home to begin filming a segment for a series called "Training Day"—essentially workout porn for fans of elite endurance sports. After grabbing footage of Cox prepping his drink bottles, we drove to Green Church Road, an undulant ribbon of asphalt with a median elevation of 7,100 feet, where we were met by Alistair Cragg, a South African-born professional runner and Cox's partner for the first part of the workout.

The pair warmed up with a few miles of easy running followed by dynamic stretches, form drills, and a handful of relaxed sprints. The workout itself was a doozy: 3 miles at 5:20 per mile (equivalent to 5:02 per mile at sea level), plus another 12 miles at marathon effort. Cox had completed the same workout 10 days earlier at an average pace of 5:16 per mile. His goal was to improve upon that number this time around.

I knew Cox was having a good day when, having completed the first 3 miles at the pace prescribed by coach Terrence Mahon, he tore through mile 4 in 4:58. "We were kind of committed at that point," he told me afterward. Cragg peeled off at 6.5 miles, leaving Cox to cover the last 8.5 miles with only a bicycle pacer (and a four-person video crew) for company. Despite the loss of his teammate, Cox did not slacken. In fact, he picked it up a notch, explaining later, "Once I hit the turnaround at 10 miles, I was like a horse smelling the barn, and I just put my head down and ground it out."

Those final miles were good television, as they say. Cox's shirt came off, his iPod came on, and his muscles tensed with effort. A red line spray-painted on the road marked the finish, where Cox stopped his watch at 1:17:09, having averaged 5:06 per mile over the final 12 miles. Clearly pleased with the outing, which he characterized as "better than expected," Cox rested briefly before cooling down.

Three weeks later, Josh Cox ran the race of his life, finishing the 2009 California International Marathon just 9 seconds behind winner Tesfaye Bekele with a personal-best time of 2:13:51, having averaged—you guessed it—5:06 per mile for the distance. If anyone was surprised by this performance, which came nearly a decade after Cox's previous best marathon, it wasn't me. Cox had been a man in command on Green Church Road, an endurance master executing his workout with a perfect blend of instinct and discipline, taking full advantage of his peppy legs without getting carried away. An athlete capable of training this expertly could only be expected to compete at the same high level.

Defeated by the Target

I thought of Josh Cox recently while witnessing a very different athlete doing a very different workout. Wayne (not his real name) came to Dream Run Camp looking to level up his competitiveness as a trail racer. I quickly realized that, to succeed in this ambition, Wayne would have to learn how to execute his workouts with the same level of command Cox had exhibited 14 years earlier.

On his third day at camp I gave Wayne a set of precision intervals, as I call them: 12 × 300 meters in precisely 85.0 seconds. The venue was a flat stretch of Kiltie Lane with a 90-degree bend in the middle—not quite as suited to precise pacing as a track would be, but that was the idea.

Wayne set off way too fast in his first interval. I know what 7:36 per mile pace looks like, and it was obvious to me that he was moving quicker than that, yet despite having the advantage of being the person doing the running, Wayne himself had no clue. He completed the rep 5 seconds (or 6 percent) too fast.

No big deal, right? Wayne had 11 more chances to trend toward greater accuracy. Alas, that trend never materialized. His last rep was no closer to the target than the first, and although he did score one bullseye, all 11 misses were on the low side, which told me that, in defiance of my clear instruction to get as close as possible to 85.0 seconds in each interval, Wayne had decided—unconsciously—to get as close as possible to this number *without exceeding it*, as I'd known he would.

How did I know? Easy: The vast majority of endurance athletes try to beat whatever target time they're given. For Wayne, an 86-second interval would have represented failure and an 84-second interval success, even though both were off target by 1 second, simply because 84 seconds is faster than 86 seconds. Endurance masters, meanwhile, try to nail their targets, and as a result they miss on the high side as often as they do on the low side, but they miss by smaller margins and score more bullseyes. Unlike Wayne, who believed he was trying to follow instructions but wasn't really, they make a fully conscious good-faith effort to execute correctly, and an experienced coach like me can see the difference from a mile away.

I noticed, for example, that Wayne glanced at his watch to check his pace at random points throughout each interval, which clearly did him no good. You really can't do much with a snapshot of your momentary pace, which is always rounded to the nearest 5 or 0 anyway. Athletes who exhibit this sort of watch dependency tend to pace erratically, speeding up when the number they see is too high and slowing down when it's too low, like a stock trader who keeps reactively selling low and buying high. An endurance master, meanwhile, would have ignored their watch mostly, except when they hit that 90-degree bend, where'd they'd have grabbed a split, allowing them to draw apples-to-apples comparisons across reps and make appropriate adjustments. Let's say their previous rep was 1.5 seconds too slow, and their split at the bend matched their time at the same point in the prior interval. In this case, the athlete would have sped up just a smidge and very likely finished right on target. There's no better way to minimize the guesswork required to succeed in a task of this sort, and athletes destined for mastery learn this on their own. The rest of us need to be taught.

I don't mean to throw Wayne under the bus. I'm just trying to show you what poor self-regulation looks like in contrast to competent self-regulation in workouts. A skeptic might consider this contrast and wonder what difference it makes. We all know Wayne could have been more precise in his pacing, but he wasn't so far off that he didn't get essentially the same physical stimulus he would have gotten from perfect pacing.

Fair point. But poor workout execution is not without consequences, even when the nature of those consequences isn't physiological. An athlete simply cannot reach their full potential without becoming an expert self-regulator, and in failing to self-regulate effectively in the workout described, Wayne manifested a general lack of ability to self-regulate, which in turned caused him to miss an opportunity to get better at self-regulating. The irony!

I should mention that among Wayne's reasons for coming to Dream Run Camp was that, by his own admission, he consistently fell short of his potential in races, hamstrung by a general reluctance to take risks in search of his true limit. I should also mention that shortly before he came to Flagstaff, Wayne—who was self-coached—suffered an episode of overreaching, a type of physiological burnout caused by failing to recognize and heed signs that he was pushing a bit too hard in training.

What difference did it make that Wayne had failed to execute a set of precision intervals precisely? It made all the difference! An athlete who can't self-regulate well enough to nail a target time in a workout is far more likely to overreach in training and underperform in races than an athlete who can. As I explained to Wayne after his workout, I don't hold athletes to a high standard of execution in training because I'm a hard-ass who enjoys imposing his own will on them. I do it because it matters. A lot.

I'm happy to report that Wayne's story ends on a hopeful note. But before we get to that, I want to tell you about another athlete, whose greatest achievement exemplifies why there is no mastery without precision, and no precision without deliberate practice.

Committed to the Target

Miho Nakata entered the IAU 24 Hour World Championships in Taipei with two goals: winning the race and breaking Camille Herron's world record of 270.116 kilometers, set at the same event four years earlier. Achieving the second goal would be a stretch for the 34-year-old from Japan, whose best performance for the duration fell 14 km short of the American's mark.

Nakata started out aggressively, averaging 7:25 per mile for the first 6 hours, and by 8 hours she was more than 2 km ahead of record pace. But she still had 16 hours of running ahead of her, and they promised to be exponentially more difficult. At the halfway point, Nakata was merely matching Herron's pace from 2019, and from there she fell behind the American's historic standard. Second winds are not uncommon in races of such extreme duration, however, and Nakata's came just in time. Minutes before the finish whistle blew, Nakata learned she'd somehow clawed her way back on track to tie Herron's record. Grimacing with effort, she put everything she had into those final minutes, sprinting stiff-legged to a new 24-hour world record of 270.363 km.

In a race that lasted a full rotation of planet earth, Nakata had beaten Herron's mark by 246 meters, or 0.09 percent. That's like racing a fellow Black Friday shopper on foot from Los Angeles to San Diego and snagging the last LEGO Enchanted Treehouse at Walmart at the exact moment your rival enters the parking lot behind you. Talk about precision!

The goal in racing is to cover a set distance in the least time possible (or to cover as much distance as possible in a set time, in the case of time-based events like the IAU 24 Hour World Championships). This is a very precise aim. An athlete either finds their absolute limit in a race or they fall short, and as Miho Nakata can tell you, differences as small as 0.09 percent can be hugely consequential.

Perfect races are rare, but they're never flukes. Most athletes never run a perfect race, and those who run one typically run more than one. What these endurance masters have that others lack is skill in the art of finding their precise limit in competition. Like any skill, this one requires practice to develop. In particular, it requires regular practice in exercising precise control of speed and effort in training.

Let's imagine that 100 runners did a set of precision intervals a week before a race. I'd bet my last dollar that the ones who executed their precision intervals most precisely would come closest to executing a perfect race one week later. It's not the numbers that matter, however; it's the control. Remember, the limit is perceptual in endurance sports. A perfectly executed race is a perfectly paced race, and pacing is done mainly by feel (i.e., perception). Performance data can be useful, but is never essential to completing a race in the least time possible.

This was shown in a study led by David Borg of Griffith University and published in the *Journal of Science and Medicine in Sport* in 2020. Thirty trained cyclists completed a pair of 20-km time trials, one with access to performance data (power output, cadence, gear ration, and heart rate) and one without. Completion times were the same in both tests, indicating that experienced athletes rely on internal perceptions to pace themselves when chasing their limit, and can take or leave data.

The point I'm trying to make is this: You have to feel your way to your limit, and your limit is extremely precise—99.9 percent is not the same as 100 percent. Gaining that last tenth of a percent requires that you to develop a finely tuned sense of effort as it relates to your limit. How is this done? Keep reading.

Intentionality and Mindfulness

Athletes in team sports like basketball, as well as those in skill-based individual sports like golf, have a particular name for the work they do to get better at their sport: *practice*. Endurance athletes, significantly, do not use this word. While basketball players and golfers talk about practice, runners and swimmers talk about *training* or *working out*—language that emphasizes the physical component of the experience and underplays the mental. With a simple mindset shift, however, endurance athletes like you can get a two-for-one, transforming workouts into practices without losing their physical benefits. All it requires is that you stop being Wayne and start being Josh Cox (figuratively speaking, of course).

The difference between a workout and a practice is *deliberateness*. An athlete can work hard without working deliberately, and that's exactly what Wayne did in his precision intervals workout. Josh Cox didn't work any harder in his marathon-pace run than Wayne did in his repeat 300s, but only Cox made a good-faith effort to execute his run perfectly, elevating it from workout to deliberate practice by approaching it *intentionally* and performing it *mindfully*.

To approach a workout intentionally is to clearly understand what perfect execution means and consciously intend to meet this standard if at all possible. Pretty basic, right? Yet athletes routinely fail to approach their workouts with true intention. In Wayne's case, a crucial sliver of daylight existed between his conscious goal of completing each 300-meter repetition in 85.0 seconds and his unconscious goal of never exceeding 85 seconds, and that's a big reason his precision intervals were so imprecise.

Even the most vanilla low-intensity training sessions are often botched due to lack of intentionality. In fact, athletes probably botch easy runs and the like more often than any other type of practice because they're so vanilla. What's the point of aiming for perfection when "good enough" will do? But even in these unchallenging, sometimes boring staples of endurance training, good enough is not good enough.

In a perfectly executed low-intensity practice, you'll never exceed your first ventilatory threshold (VT_1), which is the dividing line between low intensity and moderate and equates to the highest effort at which you can carry on a normal conversation. In principle, this couldn't be easier. Perfect execution is entirely within your control, requiring nothing more than a calculated restraint. But in my experience, athletes rarely complete an entire low-intensity training session without straying into the no-man's-land of moderate intensity. I've heard all kinds of excuses after the fact:

"My watch kept telling me to slow down, but it felt so easy!"

"I guess I did run too fast *technically*, but it wasn't by a lot."

"Yes, but my *average* pace was in Zone 2."

"It was such a beautiful day that I kept getting distracted."

"The dog ate my homework."

Okay, I haven't actually heard that last one, but it's no worse than the others. Here's what you'd say instead if I injected you with truth serum:

"I ran too fast for one reason only, which is that I never really intended to complete the entire session at conversation pace, at least not in the same way I intend to avoid straying into oncoming traffic when I'm running along the shoulder of a busy street."

You simply cannot execute a practice perfectly without having a clear and singular intention to do just that. But intentionality does not alone guarantee perfect execution. You must also be fully present while you're practicing, which is another way of saying you must perform each session mindfully. Like intentionality, mindfulness seems almost too basic to bother teaching, yet mindless training is the norm. I return again to Wayne's precision intervals workout, in particular rep number eight, which he completed in 79 seconds—his most egregious miss. On the ride back to camp, Wayne explained to me that an attractive female runner had passed him in the other direction during that particular interval, causing him to speed up. Talk about mindless!

Wayne's actual words, I believe, were: "I *had* to speed up." How revealing! They suggest a tacit belief on his part that he could not have done otherwise, as though a sudden and powerful wind had blown him forward from behind. But there was no wind, and Wayne could have done otherwise. To get him to see this, I asked him if he would have run his eighth interval 6 seconds too fast if he'd known he would be imprisoned for life if he did so.

"Probably not," he conceded.

Lucky for Wayne, poor workout execution is not a felony. It is, however, a sin—at least if you claim to want to become an endurance master. Athletes who blindly persist in C+ workout execution have no chance of reaching their full potential. True perfection is unattainable—we all know this—but that's no excuse for failing to aim for it. Our reach always exceeds our grasp. To grasp the brass ring of mastery, which is attainable, we must reach beyond it, toward perfect.

Toward the end of his stay at Dream Run Camp, I had Wayne do a workout that was designed to develop this finely tuned sense of effort. Specifically, I had him do what I call *stretch intervals*, where the challenge is to cover slightly more distance in each interval, leaving just enough capacity in reserve to cover slightly more distance in the last interval than in the one before with an all-out effort. Executing the session perfectly demands that the athlete pay very close attention to their perceptions as they go, aiming to run the first interval at an effort that leaves just enough capacity for a certain number of incremental increases.

The exact number of intervals I assigned Wayne (eight) didn't matter. I could have given him seven intervals or nine and it would have made no difference to his fitness, just as it makes no difference whether a bomb misses its target by ten yards or twenty. Same thing with the duration of each interval (30 seconds). I could have made the intervals shorter or longer, and Wayne would have arrived at his next start line with the same amount of potential. But in trying as hard as he could to cover slightly more distance in each interval, Wayne did something that would measurably increase his chances of finding his true limit in a future race.

I'm happy to report that Wayne acquitted himself fairly well in his stretch intervals, failing only once in eight attempts to cover more distance than he did in the preceding intervals. Not a bullseye, but a sign of hope for him—and for you.

FROM PRINCIPLE TO PRACTICE

Perfect races are only executed by athletes who routinely aim for perfection in practice through intentionality and mindfulness. Here are three ideas on how to apply this lesson in the days, weeks, and months ahead:

1/ Before your next training session, consider what it means to execute that session perfectly, and take this understanding into the workout. If it's an easy run, for example, identify the heart rate, pace, or power that is associated with the upper limit of your low-intensity range (i.e., the first ventilatory threshold) and vow not to exceed this number at any point during the session.

2/ Begin a habit of assessing your execution after each workout. Take stock of what you did well and what you could have done better. Don't beat yourself up unfairly for falling short of perfection, but at the same time, don't lower your standard below perfection. Remember, our reach always exceeds our grasp. To achieve your best, you have to strive for perfection.

3/ Spice up your training with novel workouts that force you to execute more mindfully. You saw two examples in this chapter: precision intervals and stretch intervals. Here's another: blinded fartleks, which entail surging for a certain amount of time (e.g., 1 minute) at a specific pace (e.g., 5K race pace) *without consulting your watch*. With practice, you'll get better at measuring time and speed by feel.

Extended Health

When I started running in the mid-1980s, only hardcore endorphin junkies knew what VO_2 max was. We read the books that cited the studies showing that peak oxygen consumption during intense exercise (i.e., VO_2 max) predicts performance better than any other indicator. In 1987, for example, researchers at NASA's Lyndon B. Johnson Space Center tested 50 male runners of varying ages and abilities and found a correlation coefficient of 0.63 between VO_2 max and running performance, meaning peak oxygen consumption alone accounted for more than 60 percent of individual differences in marathon times.

Today, thanks to podcast influencers like Dr. Peter Attia and the Zone 2 training trend, even the most casual athlete is aware that adding horsepower to the aerobic engine supercharges performance like nothing else. But the real mainstreaming of VO_2 max happened when health-conscious senior citizens learned that aerobic capacity is also among the strongest predictors of longevity. An ambitious 10-year study published in the *European Journal of Preventive Cardiology*

TABLE 10.1 **Health and Fitness Effects of Endurance Training**

EFFECT	HEALTH BENEFIT	FITNESS BENEFIT
Increased aerobic capacity (VO$_2$ max)	Increased longevity	Greater endurance performance
Improved cardiac function	Reduced risk of cardiovascular disease	Greater endurance performance
Stronger muscles	Reduced fragility	Greater speed, power, muscular endurance
Improved endocrine function	Better mood state, better sleep, better sexual and reproductive function, etc.	Accelerated fitness gains, faster recovery
Leaner body composition	Reduced risk of metabolic diseases	Greater movement economy
Increased metabolic efficiency	Reduced risk of metabolic diseases	Increased lactate threshold, endurance
Heightened immune and antioxidant function	Reduced vulnerability to infectious diseases, reduced cancer risk	Faster recovery, increased training tolerance
Increased neuroplasticity and brain function	Reduced cognitive decline, dementia risk	Improved focus, inhibitory control, endurance
Increased bone density	Reduced risk of fractures	Reduced injury risk, increased training tolerance

found that VO$_2$ max was a better predictor of mortality than body mass index or frailty in a population of 552 elderly adults. Simply put, the more horsepower an older person has in their aerobic engine, the less likely it is that person will die anytime soon.

We tend to think of fitness and health as two separate things—related but distinct. But the fact that VO$_2$ max is correlated with both endurance performance and longevity suggests otherwise. And the overlap between fitness and health goes well beyond aerobic capacity. Table 10.1 summarizes the effects of endurance training on a variety of bodily organs and systems and how these effects benefit both health and fitness.

As you can see, pretty much everything endurance training does to the body elevates health and fitness equally, which tells us that health and fitness aren't merely related but the same. People often say that health is the foundation of fitness, implying that fitness is something we layer on top of health, adjacent but separate, when in reality fitness is just *more health*. One scoop of endurance training, so to speak, gives you health. Two scoops give you fitness.

Not every athlete understands this. Believing they can pursue fitness independently of health, many bargain their health away in exchange for a false promise of greater fitness. Common traps are restrictive eating, overtraining, and obsession—three ways of chasing fitness that often pay short-term dividends but always cause long-term erosion of health, and when health erodes, so does fitness. My three rules for avoiding these traps are:

1 / Train for tomorrow.
2 / Eat like your great-great-grandparents.
3 / Be balanced.

Let's explore each of these rules.

Train for Tomorrow

It's natural to associate hard work with improvement as an endurance athlete. But although hard work is the most obvious contributor to fitness, there are many more pieces to the puzzle, and athletes who approach their training with a "more is better" mindset invariably sabotage their fitness by impairing their health.

Ryan Hall can tell you a thing or two about that. When he left his longtime coach Terrence Mahon in 2010 to become self-coached, Hall was unquestionably the greatest male distance runner in the United States, having finished third in the Boston Marathon the prior year and having set the American record in the half-marathon in 2007. But in 2012 he decided it would be a good idea to attempt to break the marathon world record at the Olympic Games in London, and he prepared for it by completing long solo training runs at world-record pace. The result was a hamstring injury that forced him to abandon the race at 11 miles, and he was never the same. After withdrawing from the 2013 Boston Marathon and the 2014 New York City Marathon and dropping out of the 2015 Los Angeles Marathon, Hall retired from competitive running in 2016, citing chronic fatigue and low testosterone, both common signs of overtraining. He was 33 years old.

"I see within myself [a] desire for quick results," Hall wrote on his blog near the end. "I'm tired of making that mistake." Sara Hall, meanwhile, avoided duplicating her husband's mistake, training for tomorrow instead of today, and was rewarded with impressive longevity, setting her own American record in the half-marathon at age 39.

A good description of "training for tomorrow" comes from another American record holder, Emily Sisson, who clocked 2:18:29 at the Chicago Marathon in 2022 and is coached by Ray Tracy, a venerable developer of collegiate and elite talents who believes that without health there can be no fitness. In a 2019 interview for *Athletics Illustrated*, Sisson said of her coach, "Ray is very conservative with everything and really stresses staying healthy so you can continue training without taking weeks or months off. So he's big on staying on top of the little things, taking a day off if you're not feeling well or have a little niggle in your foot or leg. He knows that in the long run the workouts aren't the be all and end all; it's more important to get out and run every day, consistently, for a long time. That consistency is what really brings improvement."

Be like Sara Hall or Emily Sisson, not Ryan Hall, and train for tomorrow, not today.

Eat Like Your Great-Great-Grandparents

Perhaps the most common way in which athletes sacrifice their health in pursuit of fitness is undereating. Convinced that lighter is better, they reduce their food intake to a level that is insufficient to support the energy demands of intensive training, a condition known as relative energy deficiency in sport, or RED-S. A notable victim is Jake Riley, who was the first American finisher at the 2019 Chicago Marathon and placed second at the 2020 US Olympic Trials Marathon before deciding to cut calories in an effort to shave weight. The results were disastrous. Riley finished 29th at the 2021 Tokyo Olympics, started only three races in all of 2022, and failed to complete the 2024 Olympic Trials.

For every Jake Riley who destroys his career by undereating, many more athletes undercut their health in search of fitness through less extreme dietary measures, including carbohydrate restriction, food group elimination, intermittent fasting, and heavy reliance on dietary supplements. It's important for all athletes to understand that, with few exceptions, the most successful performers don't do any of these things. I wrote about how the world's greatest endurance athletes eat in *The Endurance Diet*. My research entailed traveling all over the world, eating with Olympic-level runners from Kenya and Japan, Dutch cyclists, Canadian cross-country skiers, Brazilian triathletes, and others. Unsurprisingly, I discovered that Kenyan runners, being Kenyan, ate a lot of *ugali*, whereas Dutch cyclists, being Dutch, ate a lot of bread. Beneath these superficial differences in food selection, however, I found striking similarities. The typical diet of an elite endurance athlete has four characteristics:

Cultural normalcy. Top athletes eat like where they're from.
Well-rounded. Far from restricting macronutrients or eliminating food groups, the best athletes eat a balance of everything.
Minimal processing. Elite endurance athletes eat natural versions of all food types, for example eschewing refined grains in favor of whole grains.
Intuitive. Whereas nonathletes tend to eat too much and amateur athletes often eat too little, champions eat just the right amount by listening to their bodies.

In short, elite endurance athletes today eat like everyone did several generations ago, when ketogenic diets and intermittent fasting didn't exist. Why? Because eating like their great-great-grandparents makes them healthier, and a healthier athlete is a fitter one. In 2019, researchers at Saint Louis University placed 11 recreational runners on each of two diets—a standard Western diet and an old-fashioned Mediterranean diet, which has all of the traits of the eating habits of world-class endurance athletes—for four days, conducting 5K time trials before and after each four-day period to test the effects. On average, the runners finished 6 percent (or 1 minute and 50 seconds) faster after eating like the elites (more or less) than they did after eating like your neighbor. And although health markers weren't measured in this particular study, it's highly likely that the performance boost associated with the Mediterranean diet was mediated by its known health effects, which include better sleep and favorable changes in gut bacteria.

Granted, athletes like Jake Riley, who overthink their dietary choices, aren't eating like your neighbor. They're counting calories, skipping meals, eliminating food groups, balancing macronutrients, and taking supplements. But it's best not to take your cues from flash-in-the-pan athletes who ride the restriction train to a few good races and are never heard from again. Instead take them from those who, like the champions I ate with (and like your great-great-grandparents), reach the top and stay there.

Be Balanced

Over the years I've encountered a handful of athletes who were completely obsessed with their sport and didn't care about anything else. All of them have been unhappy as people and erratic as athletes. This is not a coincidence. Athletes who have no life outside of training and competing are almost always unhappy and erratic. When a person's identity becomes enmeshed in a single avocation, their happiness becomes dependent on how things are going. If they have a bad workout, they have a bad day. And let's be honest—a person has to be a little unbalanced emotionally in the first place to become this unbalanced in their life, and when an athlete is unbalanced emotionally, they have a lot of bad workouts.

In the 1980s, psychologist Patricia Linville gave the name "self-complexity" to this phenomenon. A person is said to be self-complex when they are multifaceted in their identity, standing apart from those who—like athletes who eat, sleep, and breathe their sport—allow a single identity to define them. Research on self-complexity has shown that well-rounded people have better coping skills than one-dimensional individuals. A 2013 study by Michelle Slone and Ilan Roziner of Tel Aviv University found that self-complex adolescents fared better emotionally after exposure to political violence than their least self-complex peers. Sports coping has lower stakes, but the underlying psychology is the same. Athletes who have a life outside of sports are better at dealing with the challenges and setbacks that occur within it.

This seems to fly in the face of the notion that high-performing athletes are singularly focused on their sport. A closer look at the science reveals that there are two distinct varieties of sport obsession, only one of which is detrimental. *Harmonious passion* applies to those who experience a strong internal desire to do something they love because they love it. "With harmonious passion," write the authors of a 2007 paper on passion and performance attainment in sport, "the passionate activity is in harmony with other aspects of the person's life. It does not hold an overpowering space in the person's identity." Not to be confused with harmonious passion is *obsessive passion*, where the drive to engage in a sport comes from contingencies such as self-worth and social acceptance. Obsessively passionate athletes work just as hard as harmoniously passionate athletes, but they have less fun doing it because their sense of fulfillment is dependent on outcomes and not woven into the pursuit of excellence as it is for the harmoniously passionate. There's also a performance disparity between the two types, with obsessively passionate athletes tending to set fear-based goals (in essence, playing not to lose instead of playing to win) that are a known drag on performance.

The ironic lesson from these findings is that the more you care about your sport, the more you should care about things other than your sport. "In other words," wrote the authors of the study mentioned above, "one can be a high-performing athlete and lead a balanced, happy life at the same time."

Health and More Health

The first 200 men to break 4 minutes in the mile have lived 4.7 years beyond their predicted life expectancy. That's according to a 2024 study published in the *British Journal of Sports Medicine*, and it aligns with previous research, including a 2022 study from the same journal, which reported that male and female Olympic athletes from the United States outlived their peers in the general population by 5.1 years.

People don't go to the Olympics to live longer, however. They go to the Olympics in search of the absolute limit of their athletic ability. But because endurance fitness and health are two facets of a single phenomenon, these athletes get a two-for-one—except when, hungry for quick results, they take shortcuts that may sometimes yield extra fitness in the short term but invariably sabotage fitness by eroding health in the long term.

Don't be this athlete. Sure, you might still live an extra five years if you adopt a restrictive diet or train like Ryan Hall or allow your athlete identity to define you, but you will not master your sport. You can't win a race you don't finish, and like it or not, you cannot be fitter than you are healthy. Wherever you get your instruction, get it from folks who know this.

FROM PRINCIPLE TO PRACTICE

Endurance fitness is an extension of general health, but it's unwise for an athlete to chase fitness at the expense of health. If you hope to reach your full potential, consider implementing the following suggestions:

1/ Take a minute to consider how much fitness and performance matter to you relative to health. We all care deeply about our health, of course, but some of us care even more about our fitness and performance, and that's fine. It's a personal choice. But regardless of priorities, every athlete must put health before fitness *in practice* to achieve their best, and all benefit from having a clear understanding of their priorities. What are yours?

2/ Take inventory of your instructors—the people who tell you how to train, eat, and use your mind to get better. Coaches, trainers, physical therapists, mentors—you know who your instructors are. It's possible that you yourself are your own primary instructional source in one or more areas. That's fine—add yourself to the list. And when the list is complete, evaluate how well each source meets your health and fitness priorities. Understanding that it's okay to value fitness and performance immensely, as long as you prioritize your health in pursuit of these things, identify mismatches between your values and your actions.

3/ Make a plan to get your priorities better aligned with the measures you take to get where you want to go. Don't just think it; write it down. Then act.

UNDERSTANDING
Why It Works

—

We now turn our attention to the third pillar of endurance mastery, understanding, but this doesn't mean you're done learning. It just means you're ready to learn the *why* behind the instruction you receive so you can be empowered to make more and better decisions for yourself.

In this section you will cultivate mastery with five lessons that deepen your understanding of endurance sports:

11

It's helpful to maintain a broad view of what works and what doesn't and how the various training components should be prioritized.

12

Subjective perceptions matter more than objective metrics in assessing how things are going.

13

You'll make more progress from month to month and year to year if you train one eye on short-term fitness building and the other on long-term athletic development.

14

Keeping things as simple as possible in your training will reduce the number of missteps you take and accelerate your progress.

15

Each athlete has their own optimal training formula, and discovering yours will require that you treat the training process as an ongoing experiment.

First Things First

Once upon a time there was a runner named Bill. He came to running later in life, after retiring from a long and successful career as a college softball coach. It's hard to think of two sports more unalike than softball and running, and despite decades of experience in the former, Bill just couldn't wrap his head around the latter. At the time we met, he'd run two marathons, aiming to break 4 hours in each, and had failed to break 4:40 both times. Convinced he could do better, Bill blamed his training.

"I've read a slew of books on how to train," he told me, "including a couple of yours. All this stuff about zones and lactic acid and periodization gets all jumbled up in my head. I go outside to do one of the workouts in the plan and instead I just run, no structure, no purpose."

Bill's no dummy. The problem for him wasn't thickheadedness but a combination of age, inexperience, and isolation. At 61, Bill had been running competitively for just two years, and he did everything alone. Running terminology was like a foreign language to him. Imagine waiting until your seventh decade on earth to learn Greek—without a teacher!

Talking with Bill got me thinking. What he needed was a clear explanation of what works and what doesn't in training—what's important and what isn't. If you ask me, there's no higher priority in the understanding phase of athlete development. The rest is details. And I knew just where to find the clear explanation Bill yearned for. In a 2016 lecture, exercise physiologist Stephen Seiler introduced Seiler's Hierarchy of Endurance Training Needs, an infographic that ranks the most impactful training methods in an eight-level pyramid similar to psychologist Abraham Maslow's famous hierarchy of human needs, where the bottom level represents the greatest need, the next level up identifies the second-greatest need, and so on.

The way to think about Seiler's pyramid as an athlete is that if you're currently not meeting any of the eight needs—in other words, if you're doing absolutely everything wrong, or you aren't doing anything at all—you should start at the bottom and work your way up. As a practical matter, you can and perhaps should jump right in and do all eight things simultaneously, but there's little point in getting the eighth-ranked need (a properly executed pre-race taper) right if you're neglecting the first-ranked need (high training frequency and volume). Norwegian triathlon coach Olav Bu said it well: "Start with the things that make up the minutes, then the seconds, then the tenths of a second."

Let's now work our way up the pyramid together, putting first things first.

1 / Total Frequency or Volume of Training

Elite endurance athletes today train at high frequency (lots of workouts) and high volume (lots of time working out). Prior to the 1960s, elite athletes trained less, and they were a lot slower. Coincidence? That seems unlikely. Even among today's elites, increased training volume is associated with greater improvement from early career to career peak. All available evidence tells us that training at high frequency and high volume is an absolute requirement for maximizing endurance fitness and performance—at least for the elites.

But what about everyone else? Until recently, there wasn't much evidence that training a lot was important for non-elite athletes. It's difficult to design a controlled study to determine the long-term influence of training volume on fitness and performance. But who needs a controlled study when technology now allows us to gather vast amounts of data from everyday athletes and look at how volume and performance correlate? A 2020 study conducted by heart rate monitor manufacturer Polar found that, within a population of more than 14,000 runners, those who ran the most performed the best in races, and those who increased their mileage the most showed the greatest improvement.

There's such a thing as training too much, obviously, and the amount of training that today's elites do would be too much for most athletes. Each of us must find our own sweet spot. But the sweet spot is always on the high side, with extensive daily aerobic workouts being both feasible and beneficial for nearly all athletes regardless of age, experience, or health status.

2 / High-Intensity Training

It's important to point out that training a lot is feasible only if most of your training is done at low intensity. That's because low intensity is vastly more sustainable than high intensity, allowing you to go longer without generating unacceptable levels of bodily stress. Low-intensity exercise also requires less recovery time, allowing you to train more frequently.

If training a lot were all that mattered, however, elite athletes would do *all* of their training at low intensity. Instead, they do modest amounts of high-intensity exercise and content themselves with slightly lower training volumes than they could sustain if they did everything easy. The reason is that high intensity improves endurance fitness in ways that low intensity does not, and when combined with lots of low-intensity work, it improves endurance fitness to a greater degree than training entirely at low intensity would do.

3 / Training Intensity Distribution

Sitting between low intensity and high intensity is moderate intensity, which is also a universal feature in the training of elite endurance athletes and offers benefits that neither low intensity nor high intensity can fully replicate. It's clear, then, that training must include all three intensity ranges—low, moderate, and high—to yield maximal fitness and performance. But what are the right proportions?

We turn again to the elites. With striking consistency, elite cyclists, runners, swimmers, and triathletes do about 80 percent of their training at low intensity and the remaining 20 percent at high intensity, while elite cross-country skiers and rowers do about eight out of every ten training sessions at low intensity and dedicate the remaining two to moderate- and high-intensity work. It so happens that Stephen Seiler was first to observe this cross-disciplinary pattern, which has become known as the 80/20 rule of intensity balance.

The word "rule" implies that athletes must maintain a precise 80/20 intensity balance all the time to maximize results, but this is not the case. It's more accurate to say—based on real-world elite practices—that athletes should maintain an approximate 80/20 balance most of the time. But considering that the average non-elite athlete does less than 50 percent of their training at low intensity, it's not a bad idea to treat the 80/20 rule as gospel, at least initially, when you're breaking existing bad habits.

4 / General Periodization Details (Annual)

The term *periodization* refers to the practice of evolving your training in goal-specific ways. Elite athletes don't train the same way year-round. While it's true that they *almost* always train at high frequency and volume, incorporate high-intensity workouts, and maintain an approximate 80/20 intensity balance, they change up the details depending on where they are in the process, and in particular on how close they are to their next important race. Periodization is necessary for the simple reason that athletes cannot indefinitely sustain the workloads required to achieve peak performances. Athletes at all levels perform best when important races are preceded by brief periods of manageable but not sustainable "overload" training, which in turn are preceded by patient buildups.

While acknowledging its importance, Seiler describes general periodization as "likely overrated" because there's more than one effective way to go about it. Some athletes periodize with a speed phase followed by a tempo phase and others with a tempo phase followed by a speed phase, while still others blend their speed and tempo training together in a single phase with changing emphases, yet all get similar results provided their overall training becomes more challenging as they move closer to the big race.

5 / Sports-Specific and Micro-Periodization Schemes

According to Seiler, micro-periodization—or how athletes string together workouts from day to day—has a "likely modest" effect on fitness. For example, it doesn't appear to matter much whether an athlete schedules lighter "recovery" weeks every third week or every fourth week or reduces their training load only when they feel the need. Nor does it seem to matter how often athletes take rest days. Once a week works for many, but most elites rest less often. An exception is Swedish speed skater Nils van der Poel, who, after winning two gold medals at the 2022 Beijing Olympics, revealed that he routinely took two consecutive days off from training every week (after cramming 32 hours of training into the preceding five days). So, that's an option as well.

What does matter is that you balance hard work and rest/recovery in such a way that your body neither accumulates excessive fatigue over extended periods of time nor loses fitness between batches of harder work. As with general periodization, though, there's more than one way to achieve this balance.

6 / Training-Stimuli Enhancement

The intriguing phrase "training-stimuli enhancement" refers to practices that enhance the benefits of training by making it somewhat harder. Examples are training at high altitude, training in the heat, and training in a fasted state. Seiler believes that such measures can make a difference, but are "individual and condition-specific" in their effects. With a nod to Olav Bu, I reserve these challenges for athletes who have mastered the basics and remain hungry to improve.

7 / Pacing Training

The fittest athlete does not always win the race. Sometimes, it's the athlete who gets the most out of their fitness on race day thanks to superior execution. In endurance sports, the most important component of execution is pacing, or the art of holding back just enough throughout the race to reach the finish line before exhaustion. As the guy who wrote *How to Run the Perfect Race*, I can tell you it's hard to run the perfect race, and studies indicate the average runner would finish up to 15 percent faster in races with better pacing. The good news is that working on pacing in training can improve your pacing on race day. Seiler rates this practice as "potentially decisive if everything else is done right."

I myself place a heavy emphasis on pacing skill development in my coaching, not only because I agree with Seiler but also because I regard pacing as a gateway to improving athletic self-regulation more broadly. The two keys to accelerating pacing skill development, I have found, are getting athletes to really focus on pacing as they train, often in gamified ways that make the process fun, and inviting them to help me evaluate their execution after workouts and races, together mining the experience for useful learnings.

8 / Training Taper

Tapering is the practice of altering your training prior to competition to ensure you're rested—but not *too* rested—and physiologically primed for a maximal effort. Seiler rates tapering as "potentially decisive if you have one isolated competition . . . and everything else is done right."

Both scientists and coaches have experimented with a variety of tapering approaches, and there's broad agreement that the optimal taper begins two to four weeks before race day, with longer tapers being more appropriate for athletes who train at higher volumes; entails a gradual, steady reduction in volume while frequency is maintained (i.e., the number of workouts stays the same but individual sessions get shorter); and includes modest amounts of work at high intensity, which all too many athletes foolishly eliminate on the mistaken assumption that doing so will leave their legs "fresh" for race day.

The Rest Is Details

Remember Bill, the latecomer to running who felt stymied by his cluelessness about how to train? Our initial phone conversation wasn't our only contact. Bill later spent a week at Dream Run Camp, the running retreat I operate in Flagstaff, Arizona. On his first day there, I sat him down and walked him through Seiler's Hierarchy of Endurance Training Needs. We spent much of our remaining time together discussing the very same ideas I've just discussed with you. Bill left the camp with a clear understanding that effective training is really quite simple, comprising eight general methods that have proven yet unequal benefits and allow for some flexibility in their implementation. Six months later, Bill completed the California International Marathon in 3:58—two minutes faster than his goal time. True story.

FROM PRINCIPLE TO PRACTICE

There are eight general training methods that are proven to benefit fitness and performance, which are prioritized on the basis of relative impact. Here are three ideas for turning this principle into practice on the path to mastery:

1/ Identify the most impactful training method that you are not yet taking full advantage of and commit to making better use of it. For example, track your weekly intensity balance and shift it closer to 80/20 if, like most athletes, you're currently closer to 50/50.

2/ Learn more about the individual methods in Seiler's hierarchy. Interested in heat training? There's a whole chapter on it in Brad Culp's book *The Norwegian Method*. Want a better grasp of macro- and micro-periodization? They're a major focus on the 80/20 Endurance coach certification course.

3/ Work your way up the pyramid level by level, resisting the temptation to jump ahead. There's little to be gained from training at high altitude (training stimuli enhancement) if you haven't already gotten your periodization right, which in turn won't benefit you much if you haven't fixed your training intensity balance.

But How Do You Feel?

You and a friend are out running together, matching strides at a steady pace of 10 minutes per mile. Which of you is working at a higher intensity?

Trick question! Since you're both maintaining the same velocity, you're both maintaining the same velocity.

Trick answer! The correct answer to the question is that it depends. If your friend is heavier than you, then your friend is working at a higher absolute intensity. But if your friend is fitter than you, then your friend is working at a lower relative intensity. And if your friend is measuring intensity by heart rate and you're measuring intensity by pace, then your friend will start the run at lower intensity and end it at higher intensity even though you're together the whole time. Confusing, right?

The concept of intensity is not as simple or straightforward as many athletes assume. In fact, it's downright slippery. To get the most benefit from your efforts to measure and regulate intensity in workouts, it helps to understand the slippery nature of this fundamental training variable. But before I clear up your confusion about intensity, I must first muddy the picture even more.

In their 2010 book *Exercise and the Heart*, cardiologists Eric Awtry and Gary Balady defined intensity as "the amount of energy required for the performance of the physical activity per unit of time." By this definition, a 9-minute mile is not just faster but also more intense than a 10-minute mile because the energy requirement is greater. It's difficult to measure energy expenditure directly during exercise, so scientists come at it indirectly, through oxygen consumption. But the biggest contributor to oxygen consumption in workouts is not speed, it's body mass. Hence, by Awtry and Balady's definition, bigger athletes are always working at higher intensities when moving at any given rate. This goes against our intuitions about intensity, which tell us it's about movement, not mass.

Most scientists agree, which is why it's common practice to correct for body mass when measuring oxygen consumption during exercise. If you've ever done a VO_2 max test, you may recall that the result was delivered to you as a certain number of milliliters of oxygen consumed per minute per kilogram you weigh. And although bigger athletes consume the most oxygen in these tests, it's the fittest athletes who consume the most oxygen pound for pound. The average sedentary woman, for example, has a VO_2 max of around 30 ml/kg/min, whereas a typical elite female runner will have a VO_2 max of close to 70 ml/kg/min. By this standard, then, it's not the heaviest athletes but the fittest who are capable of exercising at the highest intensities.

Once again, however, our intuitions balk. If two athletes are working as hard as they can, are they not working at the same relative intensity even though the fitter athlete is consuming more oxygen? As before, most scientists would say they are, which is why oxygen consumption is most often as a percentage of an individual's VO_2 max. A novice athlete and an elite athlete who are both running intervals at 90 percent of VO_2 max are working at the same relative intensity despite the fact that the elite is running much faster and consuming oxygen at a much higher rate.

Absolute intensity numbers—such as 30 ml/kg/min—tell us who is fitter, while relative intensity numbers—such as 90 percent of VO_2 max—tell us how hard an athlete is working relative to their personal limit, and it's relative intensity that matters on a practical level. A beginner and a pro who each spend 5 minutes at 90 percent of VO_2 max will be equally challenged and gain equal benefits, though the elite will cover a lot more ground in that time by virtue of being capable of hitting higher absolute intensities.

The Blind Men and the Elephant

Here's where things get really slippery. You see, VO_2 max is not intensity itself. It is merely one way of measuring intensity. There are lots of other ways to measure intensity—including heart rate, power output, blood lactate, and perceived exertion—and they don't always tell the same story about how hard an athlete is working. This was shown in a 2022 study by researchers at the University of Kent. Seven cyclists completed a series of 30-minute indoor rides at fixed levels of perceived exertion (RPE). In half the rides, they were asked to maintain an effort rating of 13 on the 6-20 Borg Scale (moderate intensity), while in the other they were asked to maintain an effort rating of 15 (high intensity). Throughout all of the test rides, the cyclists' power output, heart rate, oxygen consumption, and blood lactate levels were monitored, along with RPE. Table 12.1 offers a summary of the results.

As you can see, the intensity of these two rides either increased, decreased, or held steady depending on which measurement you looked at. If you happened to look at heart rate or blood lactate, intensity increased in both trials. But if you looked at power, intensity decreased. And if you looked at RPE or oxygen consumption, the intensity was

TABLE 12.1 **Variability of Intensity Metrics**

	MODERATE INTENSITY 30:00 @ GET		HIGH INTENSITY 30:00 @ GET +15%
RPE	Steady at 13	←→	Steady at 15
Power	Modest decrease from 184W to 175W	↓	Significant decrease from 219W to 193W
Heart Rate	Significant increase from 144 bpm to 158 bpm	↑	Significant increase from 159 bpm to 171 bpm
Oxygen Consumption	Steady at 33 ml/kg/min (with very slight increase to 35 ml/kg/min at the end)	←→	Steady at 39 ml/kg/min
Blood Lactate	Significant increase from 2.46 $[La-]_b$ to 4.26 $[La-]_b$	↑	Significant increase from 3.36 $[La-]_b$ to 6.7 $[La-]_b$

Note: GET is gas exchange threshold, which is roughly equivalent to lactate threshold.

steady. It's beyond the scope of this lesson to explain why certain metrics increased while others decreased and still others didn't budge. What matters is that they did. And what this tells us is that intensity is not a single phenomenon but a sum of disparate factors.

It's like the parable of the blind men and the elephant. Ask a group of blind men what an elephant is, and each man's answer will vary based on which part of the elephant he's touching. Ask an exercise scientist what intensity is, and their answer will vary based on how they measure it.

Okay, fine. But you're not an exercise scientist. You're an athlete. As such, you don't need absolute epistemological certainty on the definition of *intensity*. You just need to measure and control intensity in ways that produce results. What you want to know is whether one of the many ways of measuring intensity is more useful than the others, and the answer is yes.

In endurance sports, unlike most other sports, performance is limited by psychology, not biology. We rarely encounter hard physical limits in races or workouts. We slow down or quit not when we can't continue but when we *feel* we can't. Study after study has found that objective measurements like power output, heart rate, oxygen consumption, and blood lactate can't predict when an athlete will hit the wall. But subjective effort can and does. As surprising as it might seem, the most reliable way to know how hard an athlete is working is to simply ask them.

Proof comes from a study published in the *International Journal of Sport Physiology and Performance* in 2023. Researchers at Ghent University sought to compare the validity of seven different formulas commonly used to assess workout stress. Six of these formulas based their calculations on objective data (either heart rate and power), while the seventh based its calculations on subjective data (rating of perceived exertion). Eleven cyclists completed three different structured workouts, after which the seven formulas were used to assign a stress score. The cyclists also completed a series of four 3-km time trials. (Don't you wish you'd gotten to do this?) The first time trial was done after a period of rest and served to establish a baseline. The other three time trials were done immediately after the three structured workouts, in a fatigued state.

As expected, everyone produced less power with tired legs. Cleverly, the researchers took this difference as a measure of how stressful the workout actually was. Can you guess which of the seven stress formulas best predicted the true impact of the workouts on subsequent time-trial performance?

Bingo! According to the study's authors, "Rating of perceived exertion was the only metric showing a response that was consistent with the acute performance decrements found for the different training sessions." In other words, simply asking the athletes how hard they felt a workout was resulted in not just the most accurate estimation but the only accurate estimation of how hard it really was.

Subjective effort ratings are equally reliable on broader timescales. In another 2023 study, this one published in the *International Journal of Sports Medicine*, Brazilian researchers collected perceived exertion ratings from 53 runners over one-week and four-week periods and calculated weekly and monthly subjective training loads. Meanwhile, heart rate data was used to calculate objective training loads using the standard training impulse (TRIMP) method. The researchers reported "very large" correlations between the two measures, concluding that "the weekly rate of perceived exertion and monthly rate of perceived exertion may be used for monitoring training load during prolonged periods."

There are a lot of athletes, coaches, and exercise scientists out there who don't want this to be true, and who will go on pretending that objective intensity metrics are more reliable and useful than subjective metrics. But imagine what would happen if an athlete had to choose one or the other. In the first scenario, an athlete is trained by a coach who has full access to comprehensive data from every training session—power output, heart rate, oxygen consumption, and blood lactate—but never asks the athlete how they feel in workouts and insists that the athlete follow data-driven training prescriptions to the letter without ever making any adjustments based on perceptions. In a second scenario, the athlete is trained by a coach who uses no numbers whatsoever in workout planning except for time, distance, and rating of perceived exertion, but communicates often with the athlete about how they feel. In the first scenario—if the science is right—there will be a mismatch between how hard the coach thinks the athlete is training and how hard the athlete is actually training, whereas in the second scenario there will be no such discrepancy, and as a result the athlete will be far less likely to train too hard or too easy and will get better results.

I admit that most self-coached athletes who tried to train entirely by feel would not fare very well. A less experienced athlete who is a bit overdependent on training devices might not be well enough attuned to their perceptions to go by feel successfully. But if you took all the gadgets away from an endurance master, they wouldn't miss a step, relying on their perceptions to train more or less the same without numbers. Even Olav Bu, the Norwegian coach known for his heavy use of lactate testing with champion triathletes Kristian Blummenfelt and Gustav Iden, concedes this point, telling one interviewer, "We could probably remove a lot of the tools I have today and still get to where we are."

The message here is not that athletes should ignore data and train entirely by feel. It's that perceptions should be considered ahead of all other intensity metrics in planning and executing training. Coaches should tell athletes how they are expected to feel in workouts and encourage them to make on-the-fly adjustments to ensure they feel the way they're supposed to. And athletes should communicate all relevant sensations to their coaches after completing each workout.

Self-coached athletes should also make an effort to improve their attunement to their subjective intensity perceptions. Ways to do this include blinding yourself to objective data in selected training sessions, which will force you to pay attention to how you feel; and sprinkling your training with short races and time trials that expose you to your current limits, a kind of tuning fork for calibrating perceived effort. The more trust you have in your own sense of intensity, the closer you are to reaching your full potential.

Perhaps it's not so slippery after all.

FROM PRINCIPLE TO PRACTICE

Subjective intensity measures are more reliable and useful than objective intensity measures. Here are three ideas for turning this principle into practice on the path to mastery:

1/ After you complete your next workout, sit down and write out a full description of your perceived effort at a particular moment. Try to capture what you felt in words that make you feel it all over again when you read them. After your next workout, do the same, but this time start the writing process in your mind while you're exercising. Continue this process to better focus your attention on the nuances of your effort perceptions, calibrating your internal intensity meter.

2/ Learn more about the various ways you can measure intensity in workouts (pace, power, heart rate, lactate, ventilation, and whatever else has become available between my writing this sentence and your reading it). Weigh the pros and cons of each and decide which ones to incorporate into your training and how to balance them with subjective perceptions of intensity.

3/ Start using *estimated time to exhaustion* as a subjective intensity guide. This is simply an estimate of how long you can sustain a given output. As noted in a previous lesson, high-level endurance athletes are able to predict how long they can sustain different outputs with great accuracy. By getting in the habit of consciously estimating how long you could continue at various speeds in training, you will develop a better feel for your limits and where you are in relationship to them, which is to say, you will develop a better subjective sense of intensity.

Hurry Up and Wait

Over the past 20-plus years I've given free advice to hundreds of athletes by email. I don't remember most of these interactions, but I'll never forget Bert Lamar. A professional skateboarder in his teens, world-champion snowboarder in his twenties, and semi-pro golfer in his thirties, Bert came to me as a beginner triathlete who aspired to compete at the elite level in Ironman events (a distance he'd never attempted) in his fifties. Would I help him?

I agreed to a call, wherein Bert made it clear to me that he had no interest in racing just to race but preferred to focus on developing his skills, putting off his competitive debut until he was ready to go toe to toe with the best. Never before had I encountered an athlete in whom such outlandish aspirations coexisted with such monkish patience. Yet something about Bert's approach felt wrong to me. In reflecting on and eventually finding words for what it was that felt wrong, I learned something about my own beliefs on athlete development, and that's why I'll never forget Bert Lamar.

Bert's choice to put long-term development before short-term competitive interests was based on the assumption that short-term competitive interests have no bearing on long-term development. But what I realized in coaching him was that focusing on short-term competitive interests not only contributes to long-term development as an endurance athlete but is indispensable to it.

Why? I'll tell you in a minute. But first let's nail down some definitions. I've been tossing around the word *development* as though everyone knows what it means, and that's far from true. In endurance sports, which outsiders have been known to characterize—not unfairly—as competitive exercise, *development* is closely tied to fitness. But there's a distinction. *Fitness* refers to an athlete's current functional capacity—the physiological determinants of how fast they can go and for how long. Athletes can almost always get fitter than they are at any given moment, but they can't do so continuously. That's because building fitness requires increased training, and even the most durable athlete can only increase their training for a few months at a time before they hit a ceiling where they stop getting fitter.

In most cases, this ceiling is only temporary. If the athlete takes a break and starts the process afresh, they will likely find that they are able to reach higher levels of training and fitness before they encounter another ceiling. And that, my friend, is development. Think of it as the fitness building that happens from season to season and year to year, rather than the fitness building that occurs within a season.

Because development works this way, endurance athletes must train in short-term cycles, rotating through phases of building, peaking, and resting, in order to maximize their long-term development. But this doesn't mean they have to actually race at the end of each cycle, as athletes commonly do. Or does it?

Actually, I think it does. The reason has to do with mindset. An athlete who knows they are racing at the end of a training cycle and actually cares how they perform in that race is inevitably going to train harder and with greater focus than an athlete who chooses to train in cycles for developmental reasons only and is biding their time for the full developmental process to play itself out before they start competing. A sense of urgency is required to maximize the athlete's overall rate of progress. As economist Cyril Northcote Parkinson noted in 1995, there is a natural human tendency for work to expand to fill the time allotted to complete it, a truth known today as Parkinson's Law. I am certain Bert would have succumbed to this tendency had he not taken my advice to go ahead and start racing.

What's unique about races is that they force athletes to get serious about maximizing their fitness by a certain date. To perform at peak levels, athletes must build their training load to a point where any further increase would take them beyond their body's current adaptive limit. If they stop even one step short of this limit, they will leave potential fitness untapped and have to settle for racing below their peak. And if they go so much as one step too far, they will enter a performance-killing state of overreaching. It's difficult to imagine an athlete who doesn't have a race on their calendar maintaining the discipline and focus required to thread this needle, taking their fitness right up to the edge but not over it—the stakes just aren't high enough.

The timing element is also crucial. Attaining peak fitness is not sufficient in itself to produce a great race performance. The athlete must also pace their fitness development in a manner that ensures they peak on the precise day of the event they're targeting. It's easy to get it wrong (I've done so more than once in my athletic career, peaking early and racing "stale"). But getting it wrong is good practice toward eventually getting it right—practice that athletes who train without racing miss out on.

A second and even more powerful mindset-related way in which finishing each training cycle with an important race accelerates athletic development has to do with goals. When things go well, athletes come away from a peak race having achieved a personal best—their fastest time ever for that distance. Naturally, it then becomes their goal to better that time in their next big race. In the language of complex systems theory, the goal of improving upon their personal best becomes an attractor, pulling the athlete toward an even higher level of performance.

Goals of this sort have an almost mystical potency. In a 2013 study, economists Eric Allen and Patricia Dechow found that finish times in marathons tended to cluster near round numbers such as 4 hours—evidence that these numbers function as attractors for those who affix their performance goals to them. What's more, Allen and Dechow noted that runners who finished marathons close to these round numbers were less likely to slow down and more likely to speed up in the last part of the race than were those who finished between round numbers, indicating that chasing these standards had a positive effect on performance.

While round-number goals are slightly different in nature than personal-best goals, they serve the same purpose, and experts outside of sport have taken note. In a 2015 study published in *Learning and Individual Differences*, educational psychologist Andrew Martin investigated the effects of personal-best goals on students preparing for a standardized math test. Eighty-nine elementary and secondary school students were separated into two groups, one of which was given a specific goal of improving upon the score they'd achieved in the same test the year before, while the other group was instructed simply to do their best. As you've likely already guessed, Martin found that members of the personal-best goal group showed significantly greater improvement.

The Innovation Factor

When athletes establish a performance standard by competing in a state of peak fitness and then raise their standard incrementally, they develop as athletes not only by working harder but also by figuring out how to train more efficiently and effectively at any given workload—in other words, by innovating. Scientists have intensively studied the conditions that stimulate innovation in the economic sphere, and their findings lend credence to the personal-best approach to athletic development.

The automobile industry offers one example of this. Governments around the world have created fuel efficiency and emission standards in an effort to combat climate change. The policymakers behind these standards hope and expect that they will catalyze technological innovation by automakers. But do they work? It depends. A global analysis conducted by Rik Rozendaal and Herman Vollebergh of Tilburg University found that two main factors influenced the effect of fuel efficiency and emissions standards on innovation: the size of the leap they demanded from manufacturers, and how much time they were given to hit the mandated numbers. The sweet spot that maximizes innovation occurs where automakers are required to make modest improvements and are not given a lot of time to do so—a situation that precisely parallels the one that athletes find themselves in when they train in short-term cycles and try to achieve a new personal best at the end of each.

The developmental process in endurance sports can be divided roughly into two phases, which we might call the brute-force phase and the fine-tuning phase. In the brute-force phase, athletes are reinvesting gains made through each training cycle in the next one, taking on greater and greater loads as their capacity increases. But every athlete reaches a point where they can no longer train any harder. This doesn't mean they have to stop improving, however. By continuing to pursue improvement despite having hit a ceiling of training capacity, athletes get resourceful, fine-tuning their training in ways that allow them to squeeze more performance out of the same volume and intensity of training.

The three most common ways in which mastery-seeking athletes innovate and fine-tune their training are: 1) tweaking their current practices based on what they've learned about their bodies; 2) trying new things that seem worth trying based on scientific evidence or widespread adoption at the elite level; and 3) cultivating a personal style of training that suits their preferences. We'll talk more about all of these measures in later lessons. In the meantime, there's no rule that says you can't begin fine-tuning your training early in your development, while you are still increasing your overall training capacity, but the reality is that only when you've maxed out this capacity does innovation become essential to continued development.

There's still a lot we don't know about the developmental arc in endurance sports. In 2023, an international team of researchers launched a large-scale longitudinal study involving an initial cohort of junior elite athletes, the purpose of which, as stated in a preliminary paper, was to "improve our understanding of cardiovascular adaptation to exercise versus maladaptation and pathology, [and] the limits of adaptation." We'll have to wait a while for the results, which are sure to expand our understanding of long-term endurance development, but we know enough already to offer athletes like Bert Lamar a helpful perspective on the phenomenon.

Prior case studies involving elite athletes have found that, although their VO_2 max typically peaks in their early twenties, they become more biomechanically efficient for many years afterward, allowing them to race faster without any additional aerobic might. To me, this is evidence that the aforementioned "limits to adaptation" in an athlete's cardiovascular system are not the limits to an athlete's overall development, and that further improvement is achievable through resourceful fine-tuning of training in a relentless pursuit of greater fitness and performance.

Putting aside the question of *how* endurance athletes improve over time, what is absolutely certain is that it takes many years for any athlete to fully develop, regardless of how old they are when they take up their sport. The only exceptions—and they are partial exceptions—are those who come to their sport with a relevant background of some sort. For example, a person who takes up running at age 50 after decades of avid mountaineering or participation in club-level soccer is already well along on the developmental curve despite their inexperience as a distance runner. By and large, though, athletes should expect the developmental process to take a while. In our age of instant gratification, too many of us botch our development by trying to "hack" the process or by allowing ourselves to become frustrated with the inescapable reality of its slow pace.

At the same time, optimal development also requires a short-term focus, as we've just seen. Even as you keep one eye on the future, you should act as though the clock is ticking and you've only got one shot—one race—to deliver the performance of a lifetime, and when that race is completed, act again as though you've only got one shot at delivering the performance of a lifetime, and so on. As I explained to Bert (who successfully completed his first Ironman in 2019, just nine months after we first connected), the right approach to athletic development is not exactly "hurry up and wait," but more like hurry up—and wait.

FROM PRINCIPLE TO PRACTICE

The most effective way to pursue long-term athletic development is to focus on short-term fitness building, setting a new performance standard at the end of each race cycle and aiming to raise that standard in the next one. Here are three ideas for turning this principle into practice on the path to mastery:

1/ Ask yourself whether you have already reached the limit of your training capacity or if you can train harder in future cycles through continued development. Can your body tolerate an increase in the frequency, duration, or intensity of your workouts provided you go about it sensibly? If you determine that you're still in the brute-force phase, make a plan for stepping up your training in the next cycle. For example, if you're a runner and you don't think your body could tolerate more running but you do believe you could supplement your running with some nonimpact aerobic cross-training, try that.

2/ Set a performance goal that functions as an attractor (e.g., a 4-hour marathon), stretching you beyond present limits in its pursuit. Don't worry about whether you have what it takes to achieve the goal. Find what it takes.

3/ Identify something you've learned about how your body responds to training and apply it to your training going forward. For example, you might notice that you recover faster from long endurance workouts than you do from moderate-intensity tempo workouts, and faster from tempo workouts than from speed workouts. In this case, you might restructure your training week to maximize the total work you're able to absorb without falling behind on recovery.

Keep It Simple, Stupid

I n 2015 I traveled through Kenya doing research for a book about the eating habits of world-class endurance athletes. Over the course of two weeks I dined with some of the country's top runners, interviewed sports scientists, and learned how to make ugali, a type of corn cake that is to Kenyan cuisine what rice is to Chinese cookery. I visited a number of other countries while working on *The Endurance Diet*, and nowhere was the diet so utterly simple as I found it to be in the cradle of humanity.

Have you ever eaten at a Kenyan restaurant? Chances are you haven't. They're virtually nonexistent outside the country, where traditional dishes like sukuma wiki (sauteed greens) and maharagwe (coconut beans) are judged to be rather bland. Ugali tastes like nothing, and though you can find french fries in Kenya, they're unsalted (and soggy). Kenyans prefer to let the corn and the potato do the talking. Yet I grew to appreciate the plainness of the food as my tour progressed.

On one memorable occasion, my companions and I were treated to a feast prepared by a couple who lived in the thick of the Kakamega Forest. They'd built their home by hand using materials from the land around it. Every ingredient of every dish they served, animal and vegetable, had been alive that same morning. The chicken, I recall, did not taste like chicken—or at least not like the chicken I was used to.

"What you Americans call non-GMO corn, we call corn," said a person I met in Kenya who had studied in the US. "What you call grass-fed beef, we call beef. What you call organic produce, we call produce."

The centerpiece of my sojourn was a two-day stop in Iten, the high-altitude capital of the nation's running scene. Having heard that Wilson Kipsang—the first man to run four marathons under 2:04—owned a hotel in town, I popped in to visit. Kipsang was there, and with the hospitality typical of his people, he paused his computer work and welcomed me into his office, where he served me tea and answered my questions about food. Aware that the typical Kenyan distance runner gets more than three-quarters of their daily calories from carbohydrates, I told my host that in America lots of people thought carbs were bad. Kipsang laughed.

"Our carbohydrates are better because they are simple," he said. "Yours come with a lot of . . . extras."

The word *simple* describes not only the Kenyan way of eating but also the Kenyan way of living. On my first day in Nairobi I visited the National Museum, where I watched in wonder as employees of the institution streamed out of the main building for their lunch break and sprawled on the lawn to snooze in suits and dresses. Such behavior is completely normal in that part of the world. By the end of my stay, I'd lost count of the number of people I'd seen sleeping outdoors in broad daylight, including construction workers at building sites.

Top Kenyan runners like Wilson Kipsang can afford to live anywhere, but very few choose to emigrate, preferring instead to maintain the same simple lifestyle as their neighbors. With few exceptions, they run without heart rate monitors, nourish their bodies without supplements, sleep without sleep trackers, and recover without compression boots. A typical day in the life of a professional runner living in Iten looks something like this:

6:00 a.m.	Run
7:15 a.m.	Breakfast
8:30 a.m.	Rest/nap
10:30 a.m.	Leisure (e.g., board games)
1:00 p.m.	Lunch
2:00 p.m.	Chores/errands
4:30 p.m.	Run
5:00 p.m.	Snack
5:30 p.m.	Rest
8:00 p.m.	Dinner
9:00 p.m.	Bed

The training itself also tends to be quite simple. Irish reporter Cathal Dennehy spent three days with two-time Olympic marathon champion Eliud Kipchoge in 2021, looking for the special sauce in his methodology. And he found it, titling the article he wrote for *Outside* "The Surprisingly Simple Training of the World's Top Marathoner." How simple? In a different article published around the same time, Kipchoge's longtime coach, Patrick Sang, listed every workout in Kipchoge's regular rotation. There were 10 of them—a recipe for greatness with few ingredients.

Simplicity rules as well in Ethiopia, Kenya's neighbor to the north and her great rival in the sport of distance running. In 2009 I sat down with Haile Gebrselassie, the 27-time world record breaker mentioned in a previous lesson, for a one-on-one interview at an Adidas-sponsored event in Los Angeles. I came prepared, having asked *Track & Field News* managing editor Sieg Lindstrom the night before for tips on interviewing the man who'd just lowered the marathon record to 2:03:58. His number one tip was that I lower my expectations.

"Is it a language barrier?" I asked.

"That's part of it," Lindstrom said. "English is his second language, so he puts things in simpler terms when he's speaking it. But the other part is that the Africans think about running in simpler terms anyway. I think they feel we overanalyze it and make it more complicated than it needs to be."

When I asked Gebrselassie to name his favorite workout, he answered, "Hill training is my favorite. Because that's the one that gives you a lot of problems. Pain. Breathing too much. Struggling too much." Not a word about his lactate threshold.

Runners from East Africa accounted for 47 of the 50 fastest men's marathon times in 2024, and for 45 of the top 50 women's times. Is it accidental that the world's greatest distance runners hail from the simplest elite running cultures? I don't think so.

The KISS Principle

The benefits of simplicity have been recognized for as long as human existence has been complex. Before Thoreau preached simplicity, Newton did, and before Da Vinci preached simplicity, Lao Tzu did. But a scientific rationale for keeping things simple did not appear until the 1960s, when Lockheed engineer Kelly Johnson included the KISS Principle (short for "Keep it simple, stupid!") in his "14 Rules of Management," a playbook created for the Skunk Works innovation team, which under Johnson's leadership developed the U-2 and SR-71 spy planes, among other advanced military aircraft. Themes of minimalism and streamlining run throughout the document, an ethos Johnson summarized with characteristic pithiness in a 1985 autobiography: "Skunk Works is a concentration of a few good people solving problems far in advance—and at a fraction of the cost—of other groups in the aircraft industry by applying the simplest, most straightforward methods possible to develop and produce new projects."

Johnson was right to believe that organizational simplicity yields greater efficiency and better results. In a 2019 study, consulting firm Heidrich & Struggles assigned a "simplicity score" to 500 large corporations and found that the fastest-growing organizations were 52 percent less complex than the slowest-growing organizations.

In the sports arena, simplicity offers a number of advantages over complexity. For starters, it demands fewer cognitive resources, enabling athletes to put more mental energy into their physical efforts. In another 2019 study, French researchers found that subjects fatigued more quickly in a test of muscular endurance when they were simultaneously engaged in a test of short-term memory. The harder the brain must work to plan and execute complex training recipes, the less actual training the body can do.

Complexity is sometimes necessary, but unnecessary complexity is wasteful. Kelly Johnson understood this, which is why he enforced strict limits on the size of human teams and mechanical tool sets at Skunk Works. It's also why the United States Armed Forces includes simplicity among its nine principles of war, and why computer programmers aspire to write lean code, knowing that as code bloats, bugs propagate. Engineers, war planners, computer programmers, and athletes don't get far by denying the complexity of their environments, but they get furthest by simplifying as much as possible the process by which they pursue goals within complex environments.

Just ask Simon Whitfield, who won a gold medal for Canada in the 2000 Olympic men's triathlon before falling victim to complexity bias, or the tendency to give more credence to complex solutions than simple ones. "With all the best intentions," Simon told me in an interview for *Triathlete*, "we had made our swimming program very complex. There were constant meetings among the three coaches on deck. There were charts and heart rates and lactate levels and test sets. There was an underwater camera. We had all this knowledge. Of course this was going to work! We had a theory. We had very bright people implementing it. We had more meetings than you could shake a stick at. But at the end of the day it was just a failed model. I had been a major pusher of this approach. But a year after the Olympics I was able to swallow my pride and say that was wrong. We had totally overcomplicated it. So we swim by the keep it simple, stupid principle now." The result was another medal—silver this time—at the 2008 Summer Games in Beijing.

Complexity bias isn't the only reason endurance athletes make their training unnecessarily complicated. For many, complexity functions as a distraction from, or even as an alternative to, hard work. Suppose a magic genie appears before you and asks you to choose between two starkly different paths to achieving your full potential: the "Kenyan Way" and the "American Way." Table 14.1 outlines these two paths.

If you're like most athletes, you'll choose the American Way, finding it more attractive for reasons you aren't entirely conscious of. Unfortunately, the magic genie lied to you when he said that both paths will lift you to your full potential. The truth is that you're more likely to become the best athlete you can be if you choose the Kenyan Way. This isn't to say the individual practices listed in the right-hand column lack value. What I am saying is that, collectively, these practices tend to come at the expense of consistent hard work. While it is theoretically possible to do everything listed in column two and still work as hard as a Kenyan, it's unlikely in practice because the main reason athletes are attracted to this kind of complexity is that they are *not* attracted to running until they almost puke!

Master the basics before you get fancy. This is my message to you, and to every athlete. If an athlete who often skips meals and eats

TABLE 14.1 **Complexity as Distraction**

THE KENYAN WAY	THE AMERICAN WAY
• Run a lot every day, mostly on dirt	• Buy an expensive sports watch and learn all of its features
• Run so hard you almost puke a couple of times every week	• Read lots of technical books about running
	• Buy expensive shoes that make running 4% easier
	• Listen to lots of running podcasts
	• Subscribe to a blood testing service that gives you tons of actionable information
	• Undergo regular physiological testing
	• Track your blood lactate, blood glucose, blood oxygenation, hydration status, heart rate variability, body composition, and sleep
	• Spend lots of time on running-related online chat forums
	• Take lots of supplements
	• Learn and execute fancy heat training and fasted training protocols
	• Purchase and use compression boots and other high-tech recovery tools
	• Follow esoteric strength and mobility training protocols designed by social media influencers
	• Etcetera

a lot of processed food asks me to advise them on practicing nutrition periodization, having heard a pro cyclist discuss the practice on a podcast, I will advise them to stop skipping meals and eat less processed food. *Then* we can talk about nutrition periodization. Not only will the athlete get more benefit from these improvements than they'll get from adjusting their day-to-day carbohydrate intake based on their training load, but they may also experience a shift in mindset that helps them choose high-value basics over low-value esoterica at other decision points.

I can't help thinking of the famous training montage from *Rocky IV,* which cuts back and forth between scenes of old-school Rocky Balboa heaving rocks and trudging through snowdrifts, while high-tech Ivan Drago lifts weights with a team of scientists around him and runs on a treadmill with electrodes pasted to him. Do you remember who wins the fight?

FROM PRINCIPLE TO PRACTICE

Unnecessary complexity hinders progress in endurance sports, and most complexity is unnecessary, as East Africa's dominant running tradition demonstrates. Here are three ideas for turning this principle into practice on the path to mastery:

1/ Assign a simplicity score to your overall process as an athlete. It doesn't have to be anything formal like the rating system Heidrich & Struggles developed for large corporations. Just take some time to look for unnecessary complexity in various aspects of your process. For example, perhaps your technology habits are too complex—you join every Strava challenge that comes along and obsess over it.

2/ Take steps to simplify your process. This could entail paring down your running shoe collection, reducing the number of biometrics you monitor, listening to fewer training podcasts, or something else. Let sufficient time pass, then analyze the results of the changes you've made.

3/ Now look for elements of your process that are too simple. Do you keep repeating the same basic strength workout over and over and wonder why you're not getting stronger? Is the only thing different about each week in your marathon training the distance of the long run? A certain amount of complexity is necessary to make endurance training truly progressive, and in my experience, most non-elite athletes train too monotonously even as other elements of their process are too complex. Take steps to break out of any simple ruts you're stuck in.

Hot and Cold

n 1802, English theologian William Paley released a book titled *Natural Theology or Evidences of the Existence and Attributes of the Deity*. Written in the thick of the scientific revolution, it was the first major attempt to prove God's existence through empirical reasoning instead of leaning on faith as theologians had always done prior to the discoveries of heliocentrism and dinosaur fossils. The book begins with the famous watchmaker analogy, where Paley argues that, because an instrument as complex as a pocket watch could not exist except as the work of a sentient creator, it follows that living organisms as complex as humans and plants could not exist without a sentient creator—namely God—behind them.

In 1986, evolutionary biologist Richard Dawkins published a refutation of so-called intelligent design explanations of life's complexity, including Paley's. With a direct nod to Paley, Dawkins titled his book *The Blind Watchmaker*, arguing that Darwin's theory of natural selection is fully capable of explaining the emergence of complex organisms without reference to a conscious author. Simple organisms become complex over vast periods of time, Dawkins explains, through a combination of random mutation, where genetic "errors" that occur in the reproductive process yield novel traits such as immunity to certain pathogens; and natural selection, where traits that help a species survive are passed on to future generations, while those that harm survival chances are weeded out. Among the examples Dawkins cites is the camera eye, an organ so complex and well-suited to its purpose that it sure seems like something that someone created versus something that just happened on its own. But in fact, the eye as we know it started off as a simple, unicellular light-sensing mechanism in ancient species, which subsequently evolved, through random mutation and natural selection, into a light-capturing mechanism, and so on, until we ended up with the sophisticated visual organs we now use to recognize faces and design websites. The watchmaker is not God but nature, Dawkins concludes, and nature is blind, creating vision (and everything else) without any vision of its own, much less intelligence, relying instead on the selective aggregation of chance mutations to generate beings of ever greater complexity.

Whether you prefer creation or evolution as an explanation for biological complexity, what is undeniably true is that evolutionary processes are happening all around us, and these processes do indeed operate blindly for the most part. Endurance training is one example. We have seen how best practices in endurance training evolved over time, with new methods emerging periodically here and there, proving their superiority in the cauldron of elite competition, then quickly diffusing throughout the global population of elite athletes, displacing prior best practices. The whole thing appears quite intentional given how much faster athletes have gotten across generations. But it wasn't intentional. Much like the gene mutations that spur biological evolution, the methodological innovations that have slowly optimized endurance training over the past one and a half centuries were standalones, each contributed by one or more individuals who had no master plan for the process as a whole and no clue where it was all going. Even today, none of us can foresee how training methods of the future will differ from today's best practices.

What we can foresee is that future training methods will not be drastically different from today's best practices. That's because we've largely figured out how to train most effectively for endurance performance. From an evolutionary perspective, 150 years is the blink of an eye. While the human species continues to evolve, our physiology today is little different from that of our forebears of the mid-19th century, when the quest to identify the best way to train for endurance began in earnest. Training methods can't just keep getting better forever like cellphones. Once we've figured out how to get the most out of the human body in its present form, no further innovation is possible until and unless the species itself changes.

Athletes living today are fortunate beneficiaries of the many useful discoveries made by clever and creative endurance seekers of the past. From them we have inherited a set of training methods that work better than all known alternatives, whether you're a 25-year-old Olympian with a VO_2 max of 74 ml/kg/min or a 55-year-old beginner with a VO_2 max of 37. These universal best practices provide a reliable starting point for all athletes—regardless of age, sex, ability, or experience—in the journey toward fulfillment of potential.

A starting point, mind you, not an end point. After all, each athlete is unique, genetically and otherwise. Therefore, no two athletes can reach their full potential with precisely the same training formula. Universal best practices such as training at high volume and maintaining an approximate 80/20 intensity balance will take us perhaps 90 percent of the way to our ultimate potential, but to get the rest of the way, we must carry forward individually the same evolutionary process that produced our current best practices, and we must do so blindly, without foresight into which deviations from generic endurance training methodologies will work best for us.

It's Child's Play

Did you ever play the childhood game Hot and Cold? An object is hidden by one child, and a second child must locate it. The seeker moves about randomly in search of the hidden object, and as they do, the hider says "warmer" if the seeker happens to move closer to the object and "colder" if they move away from it. In this manner, the object is inevitably found despite the seeker's "blindness."

The search for optimal training is similar. As mentioned, it began in the 19th century, when elite athletes and their coaches embarked on the process of seeking the most effective ways to train for endurance performance. The results these endurance seekers got from putting new methods to the test in competition let them know if they were getting closer to or further from the thing they sought. When they tried something different and won, they heard "warmer" and continued in that direction. When they got beaten by someone who trained differently, they heard "colder" and moved away from their losing practices.

The flaw in this analogy is that optimal training is not the same for every athlete. There is no hidden object that, once discovered, ends the game for everyone. The version of Hot and Cold that we play today has two parts. The first part is easy, consisting of nothing more than receiving best practices passed on to us by athletes of yore. The second part is much harder, requiring us to search within collective best practices to find our own individual best practices.

Imagine a grassy park with objects hidden throughout it. The space inside the park's fenced borders represents current best practices in endurance sports. Thanks to the efforts of past generations of endurance athletes, who gradually "warmed" their way to this park in the historical part of the Hot and Cold game, we today are privileged to begin the search for our own optimal training formula at the front entrance. To gain entry, we need only learn and heed the universal best practices bequeathed to us by our athletic predecessors. But somewhere within the park lies a single object that represents our own personal optimal training formula—a formula that is consistent with universal best practices but different in certain details from any other athlete's optimum. Here, the game of Hot and Cold continues. To find your hidden object, you must try things, pay attention to the results, and retain practices that seem to work ("warmer") while discarding those that don't ("colder").

In 2022, the journal *Medicine and Science in Sports and Exercise* published a study that illustrates the process I've just described. Recreational runners were separated into two groups, one of which followed a predetermined 15-week training plan while the other had their training modified twice per week for 15 weeks, based on indicators of recovery status and readiness to train (specifically, nocturnal heart rate variability, perceived recovery, and the relationship between heart rate and pace while running). Whenever these measurements indicated that an individual runner was sufficiently recovered and ready to work, their training load was increased. And when the same measurements showed fatigue or potential overreaching, the load was decreased. Both groups completed 10K time trials at the beginning and end of the 15-week training period. And while both groups saw improvement, members of the individualized training group improved far more, lowering their time by an average of 6.2 percent, compared to just 2.9 percent for the static-plan followers.

The purpose of this study was not to identify a personal optimal training formula for the individual athletes who served as subjects (an ambition that would have required a much longer study) but to test the effect of modifying training loads based on variations in training responses. Had the experiment continued, however, distinct patterns would have emerged among the 16 runners in the individualized training group, with some demonstrating a greater overall training load tolerance than others, some requiring a deloading period more frequently than others, and some showing a tendency to recover better than others from certain types of workouts—data that any competent coach could use to create more customized and effective training plans for each runner.

Keep in mind, this is just a single example. There are innumerable ways in which one athlete's optimal training formula might differ from another's. I've coached some athletes who could handle a lot of volume but had a limited tolerance for hard workouts, and I've worked with others who exhibited the opposite pattern. I've coached some athletes who thrived on long endurance sessions and others who crumbled under them. I've coached some athletes who benefited from a heavy emphasis on strength training and others whose endurance training was negatively affected if they did more than a minimal amount of gym work. I'll stop there, but I could easily continue.

All of this might seem rather intimidating. As an athlete, how are you supposed to identify your personal optimal training formula when there are so many possibilities? Relax. Remember that using universal best practices as a starting point takes any given athlete—including you—90 percent of the way to their full potential. And though it isn't easy to figure out the remaining 10 percent of your formula, if you go about it sensibly, you can make continual progress. There are four main components of endurance fitness in which individual differences show up:

1 / Speed (measurable as performance in a 10-second sprint)
2 / VO_2 max (measurable as performance in a 6-minute time trial)
3 / Threshold fitness (measurable as performance in a 20-minute time trial)

4 / Endurance (measurable as the rate at which speed or power degrades between a 6-minute time trial and a 60-minute time trial)

With each of these four basic components of endurance fitness, there are a few ways in which individual differences can manifest:

Strengths and weakness. Are you stronger or weaker than other runners of similar overall ability in terms of speed, VO_2 max, threshold fitness, and endurance?

Responsiveness. Does a little bit of speed, VO_2 max, threshold, or endurance training go a long way for you, or not so far?

Tolerance. Does more than a little bit of speed, VO_2 max, threshold, or endurance training tend to put you in a hole, or not so much?

Consider what you learn in these four key areas against the backdrop of the specific demands of the races you do and the specific type of fitness demanded by these events. Now you're ready to play Hot and Cold: The Athlete Edition!

In my case, the Hot and Cold Game began in my mid-thirties in response to three problems affecting my efforts to reach my full potential: 1) frequent injury, 2) occasional overreaching, 3) a tendency to hit the wall in longer races. Learning and following general practices had given me a solid foundation and yielded some good race performances, but to develop any further, I needed to find my own way forward. So I did, evolving a more individualized training approach by experimenting on myself in a controlled way. Switching to an "always almost ready" approach to race preparation, where the focus was more on consistency than on ramping up, reduced my injury rate significantly. Deemphasizing high-intensity intervals and doubling down on longer efforts at moderate intensities cured my susceptibility to overreaching. And a variety of measures, including more frequent long runs (I sometimes ran back-to-back 20-milers on the weekend), longer long runs (more than once, I ran a 50K in training before racing a marathon), and depletion runs (long runs undertaken in a fasted state) put an end to my late-race bonking.

I share these specifics not because I think you should emulate them but merely to illustrate the right approach to finding the optimal training formula for an individual athlete, which is to treat the process as an ongoing experiment. With this approach, you're never simply *doing* things but rather always *trying* things. You're blind to where it's all going, but that's okay. There's no need to know what will work before you try it because you can easily identify what is working once you've tried it. And from there, all you have to do is retain what works, discard what doesn't, and continue to try stuff. That's how the blind watchmaker created all of the beautiful life around you, and it's how athletes like you can reach your full potential.

FROM PRINCIPLE TO PRACTICE

It is impossible to deduce the most effective way to train for endurance—it can only be discovered through experimentation and learning. Here are three ideas for turning this principle into practice on the path to mastery:

1/ Identify your primary limiter—the one problem or challenge that stymies your progress more than any other. Ask yourself, *When I fail, why do I fail?* Then ask yourself, *What am I currently doing to overcome this limiter, and what might I be doing that I haven't done already?* Don't be afraid to think outside the box. Say your primary limiter is a feeling of weakness in your legs in the later stages of races, and you wonder if running with a weighted backpack or doing squats and lunges between high-intensity run intervals might make a difference. Neither method is widely practiced in the higher echelons of the sport, but they're not crazy ideas, and there's no harm in testing them out. If you're stuck for ideas, consult a coach or experienced fellow athlete.

2/ Having identified your primary limiter and come up with a way to address it, experiment. Incorporate the new method into your training and see what effect it has. If the effect is good (warmer), keep going, but if it's bad (colder), pivot and try something else.

3/ Learn about how notable athletes have optimized their own training. There are limitless examples. One is Parker Valby, an Olympic runner who overcame a pattern of injury by adopting a training approach comprised of just three runs per week and a ton of nonimpact cross-training. Sift through such examples for outside-the-box methods that might work for you.

INDIVIDUATION

How It Works for You

—

In the field of developmental psychology, the term *individuation* refers to the process by which a person nurtures a distinct identity and sense of self. A similar process plays out in athletic development, where individual competitors become increasingly self-guided as they move toward mastery. Coaches and other experts still have a role to play, but in the words of renowned multisport coach Frank Dick, "Our function as coaches is not to give ownership to those we coach; it is to create a process for them to take ownership. They are active in this, not passive."

In this section you will move toward mastery with these five lessons specific to individuation and athlete development:

16

Athletes must become active partners with their coaches in decision-making if they are to develop the self-efficacy required to attain mastery.

17

It's necessary to selectively try new things in training to forestall and disrupt complacency.

18

Athletes should put the most helpful spin possible on the challenges they face through the psychological technique of cognitive reframing.

19

Training is more effective when it is shaped in accordance with an athlete's personality and preferences.

20

Every athlete is an exception to the rule to some degree, and athletes and coaches must therefore operate as creative problem solvers rather than as rote appliers of fixed rules.

Choose Your Adventure

The athletes I coach remotely are entitled to unlimited electronic communication with me. Some take fuller advantage of this perk than others, but none takes fuller advantage than Jasmine, who also happens to be my longest-tenured client. A typical example is the time she had a bad reaction to running in hot weather. In the morning I found the following message in my email inbox, sent in response to my request that she update me after getting a good night's sleep:

Hello Matt,

I could use some guidance for today. Here's what's going on:

- I am beginning to feel okay now but struggled to recover from yesterday's run. Dehydration is a factor. I woke up thirsty at least every hour overnight.
- I should be fine to run later today but it wasn't a safe option this morning. I am prioritizing drinking lots of water.
- Unfortunately, this means running in the hottest part of the day.

- I'm looking forward to the workout but don't think it transitions well indoors.
- I can think of three options. This is a workout I really want to do, so my preference is 1 or 2 (or something better you have in mind):
    1 / Move the workout to tomorrow morning and run easy indoors today.
    2 / Do the warm-up and cooldown inside and the intervals outside (I think it could work since it's RPE-based and has walking recoveries).
    3 / Do a different workout.

What do you recommend?

The workout in question was a set of acceleration intervals: specifically, 5 × 3 minutes ascending from a moderate pace to a relaxed sprint. Not the hardest workout ever created, but challenging enough that, based on what Jasmine had written, and considering the overall context, I thought it unwise for her to go ahead with the original plan. There'd been a handful of past instances when sticking to plan had not gone well for us, and I wasn't eager to repeat the mistake. Also, it was clear which way Jasmine herself was leaning, so I advised her to just run easy and push the workout back a day.

I share this exchange (which, I should mention, was not out of the ordinary—Jasmine and I email back and forth in this manner all the time) because it is a textbook example of facilitative coaching, or collaborating with the athlete to make decisions affecting their training. When a coach-athlete relationship enters this stage, the individuating athlete begins to assume the role of expert—ready, qualified, and empowered to generate ideas and offer opinions about what to do in various situations. This is very different from the preceding stages, where athletes are focused on cultivating the motivation, learning, and understanding they need to take ownership of their journey, and where the coach does all the thinking.

Correction: *most of* the thinking. As I've said before, it's important that athletes begin to improve their self-regulatory ability from day one of their journey toward endurance mastery. The reality, however, is that newer athletes often don't feel ready to take an active role in shaping their training. One of my favorite parts of the coaching process is the transition point where an athlete begins to speak up on their own behalf. In the early days of our partnership, Jasmine played a far more passive role in the planning process. When she started sending me emails like the one I shared, I was delighted, knowing that the overall quality of our decisions would improve as a result of her more active involvement.

Too many coaches *never* bring their athletes to the individuation stage. In their eyes, allowing athletes to shape their own training is a dereliction of duty, and perhaps even a threat to job security. Of course, they couldn't be more wrong. A coach's highest duty is to guide their athletes toward full mastery of their sport, and as you know, the very definition of mastery is being able to make good decisions for oneself consistently and with confidence. As for job security, giving athletes a voice in their training is the ultimate job security for coaches.

A case in point is my friend Lauren's choice to leave her first coach, who insisted on total control of her training decisions, for a different coach who favored a collaborative approach. The first coach's autocratic style wasn't a problem initially, when an inexperienced Lauren had few opinions about her training, but as time passed, she began to chafe against her voicelessness in the relationship. In the end, there was one decision that first coach couldn't stop Lauren from making, which was the decision to fire her. Coaches like this one, who fail to nurture independence in athletes, are like parents who do the same with their children. What they end up nurturing instead are resentment, rebellion, and, ultimately, rupture.

When coaches act as facilitators with athletes, the resulting benefits are threefold. For starters, facilitative coaching fosters self-efficacy, or the belief that the athlete is able to competently steer their own training. Studies have shown that as athletes' self-efficacy rises, so does performance. Facilitative coaching also enhances trust in the coach-athlete relationship—in both directions. When athletes feel trusted by their coach, they become more trusting of their coach. What's more, better decisions are made and better outcomes are achieved when athletes participate in the process, as we saw in the example of Jasmine's email. Coaches typically have more knowledge of the sport than their athletes do, but athletes know more about what's going on in their bodies and minds and in their day-to-day lives. It's easy to understand why better decisions will be made when coaches and athletes work collaboratively, combining their respective expertise.

Facilitation is a skill, and one that is largely distinct from knowledge. A coach could know everything there is to know about their sport and still suck at empowering athletes to become better self-regulators. Likewise, a coach could know relatively little about their sport and be highly effective in moving athletes toward mastery through individuation.

In the corporate domain, coaches seldom know more than a fraction of what the executives who hire them know about their industry. That's not a problem, however, because the job of the executive coach isn't to dispense technical knowledge but to help their clients make better decisions and achieve better outcomes by facilitating better use of their own knowledge and expertise. It's the same with elite athletes, who often have more than enough knowledge to coach themselves yet benefit from having a coach who functions as a facilitator. Coincidentally, Lauren's new coach happens to be an executive coach by trade, so it's not surprising that he practices a facilitative style of coaching with her.

The Adventure Mindset

There's a particular method of executive coaching called adventure coaching that's especially relevant to endurance sports. Also known as *adventure programming*, the practice has been defined as "the deliberate use of adventurous experiences to create learning in individuals or groups." Traditionally, this type of coaching has involved immersing participants in unfamiliar outdoor challenges, then discussing them with a view toward extracting lessons that can be applied to participants' work situations. Increasingly, though, the same method is being used within the office environment, with coaches encouraging executives to approach their day-to-day work itself as an adventure, where risk and uncertainty are inherent and decision-making is never perfect but always improvable. All in all, the adventure mindset is a very useful way for coaches and athletes to approach training.

You're probably familiar with the Choose Your Own Adventure book series created by Edward Packard. In these books, the story takes a different path on each reading based on choices the reader makes before turning the page. The inspiration for this interactive reading model came when Packard was making up a bedtime story for his daughter and he ran out of ideas for what would happen next, so he asked her to decide. The creative partnership that was forged between Packer and his child is not unlike the collaborative decision-making process that unfolds between coaches and athletes, where the former offer choices and the latter choose.

There are three basic techniques coaches can use to facilitate collaborative decision-making with athletes, and they mirror the techniques Packard used in telling his bedtime stories. First, coaches need to ask questions that invite the athlete into the process. In my athlete meetings, I'm always asking things like:

What are you in the mood for next week, training-wise?
Do you feel there's anything missing from your training?
Is there something we're doing that, in your view, isn't working?

There's no guarantee the answers to these questions will be useful in any particular instance, but there's always the possibility, and that's all that matters.

Another useful technique in collaborative decision-making is offering options to athletes—allowing them to literally choose their own training adventure from among a limited number of possibilities. "I was thinking about giving you a tempo run on Tuesday," the coach might say, "because you're due for one. But with your mountain race coming up, hill repetitions might be better, except we've done a lot of them already and I'm concerned about overdoing them. Another option is a hybrid session that mixes together tempo work and some hills. What do you think?" As long as the coach is willing to stand behind all of the options they're offering, there's little risk and a lot of potential upside to this practice. In my experience, things almost always turn out well when athletes are given the opportunity to choose from a menu of carefully vetted possibilities.

The third collaborative decision-making technique I rely on in my coaching is encouraging athletes to take the initiative in decision-making and rewarding them when they do. This happened recently with an athlete of mine named Sara. She'd fallen just short of her goal in a half-marathon, and when we talked about it afterward, she told me she felt we hadn't done enough work at the high end of Zone 2 (or the upper limit of low intensity), and she wanted more in her next training cycle. While I did not entirely agree with Sara's assessment, I liked that she was proactively critiquing her training, and I wanted her to feel heard. One reason kids love Choose Your Own Adventure stories is the sense of control they have, and athletes get the same reward when their coach is responsive to their requests. In Sara's case I proposed a compromise solution of setting aside one run per week for practice at the high end of Zone 2. The following cycle went well (perhaps partly because of this adjustment, perhaps not), and when she raced another half-marathon at the end of it, Sara achieved her goal.

The surest way to benefit from the advantages of facilitation as an athlete is to work with a coach—but not just any coach. My friend Lauren is by no means the only athlete who's found out the hard way that not every coach practices a facilitative style. To avoid getting stuck with a drill sergeant, inquire before you hire, asking prospective coaches about their attitude toward collaborative decision-making and perhaps also requesting client references and asking those athletes how involved they feel in the decision-making process.

For the self-coached athlete, journaling may function as a serviceable substitute to working with a facilitative coach. I find that the act of writing promotes deeper levels of reflection than mere thinking does, and that rereading something I wrote in the past is akin to conversing with a separate person possessing a different perspective than my own. Years ago, Bill Rodgers, the legendary four-time winner of the Boston and New York City marathons, told me with respect to his training journal, "I think it's smart to constantly evaluate our physical feelings and our training efforts. It's a great way to break out of the mindless running we sometimes do. I'll look at my log and realize I'm tired, as I've trained too many days in a row without a rest day." That's a great example of self-facilitation.

Another option for self-coached athletes is to find a confidante—someone you can use as a sounding board when making training decisions. If this person is a fellow athlete with knowledge of the sport, so much the better. But they don't have to be. Remember, most corporate coaches don't know much about their clients' industries. What makes them effective is their ability to draw better decisions out of their clients by asking questions, presenting options, and rewarding good judgment, much like a parent reading a Choose Your Own Adventure story to their child.

Where will *your* story go from here?

FROM PRINCIPLE TO PRACTICE

To master your sport, you must get comfortable making decisions for yourself, with just the right amount of external support. Here are three ideas for turning this principle into practice on your path to mastery:

1/ Imagine your athletic journey is a Choose Your Own Adventure story, and the most important decision you now face is a fork in the narrative. See what effect this shift in perspective has on your approach to choosing a direction.

2/ Start a training journal if you don't already have one. And if you do have one, start rereading past entries, mining them for insights to facilitate your next training decision. In doing so, you might discover that you're in a bit of a motivational rut and it might be time to shake things up with new training stimuli, or that you've been neglecting a certain type of workout that you benefitted from in the past and ought to reintroduce it.

3/ Identify the one person in your life who best facilitates your athletic decisions, whether it's a coach, spouse, best friend, or someone else. To the extent that you collaborate with this person in making decisions about your goal pursuit, is there room for improvement? Is this person even the right person to be your primary facilitator, or should you look elsewhere? Answer these questions, then act upon your answers.

Disrupt Complacency

Sergei Bubka knows a thing or two about breaking records. The legendary Ukrainian pole vaulter set an astonishing 35 world records in his storied athletic career, the last of which stood for more than a quarter of a century. But by his own admission, he probably could have gone even higher. "Often I jump only what I need to jump to win," he told one journalist at the peak of his excellence. "If the world record were 6.2 [meters] right now, I'd jump 6.3. That is simply the way I am."

We're accustomed to thinking of performance standards as attractors, drawing athletes to new heights of performance with their psychic magnetism. World records help champion athletes set new world records by stimulating greater effort and innovation, and in the same way, personal bests help everyday athletes like us set new personal bests. But there's another side to this phenomenon, which is hinted at by Bubka's confession. I call it the *good-enough principle*—there's a natural human tendency to do what's required to achieve one's goals and no more, resisting innovation when it's not necessary to goal attainment.

The good-enough principle originated in the work of Daniel Milo, a professor of natural philosophy, whose 2021 book *Good Enough: The Tolerance for Mediocrity in Nature and Society* challenges traditional interpretations of Charles Darwin's theory of evolution by natural selection, particularly the notion of "survival of the fittest." In school we learned that certain genetic mutations are retained across generations in a given species because they produce characteristics that aid survival, while other mutations are weeded out because they reduce survival chances. While this is mostly true, Milo offers dozens of examples of species characteristics, including the giraffe's long neck, that came about by pure chance, conferring no survival advantage whatsoever, and were retained simply because they didn't harm survival chances—in other words, because they were good enough.

As you've probably gathered, I'm rather fond of analogies. Here's one that will help you understand Milo's concept of good enough, and how it applies not just to natural evolution but to other dynamic systems as well, including endurance training. The words you're currently reading were typed on a standard QWERTY keyboard (named for the first five letters on the top row of keys). Have you ever wondered why the letters are arranged this way? It was done to extend the lifespan of mechanical typewriters by evenly distributing frequently used letters, such as *E*, with rarely used letters, such as *Q*, across the keyboard. Today, mechanical typewriters are obsolete, and there are alternative ways of organizing keyboards that would significantly increase productivity. One of them, known as Dvorak, has been shown to increase output by as much as 60 percent. Yet these alternatives will never garner mainstream adoption because QWERTY is considered good enough, or at least not sufficiently bad enough to justify the disruption of executing a wholesale shift to Dvorak or some other keyboard arrangement.

Oftentimes people need to be forced to innovate by events beyond their control that disrupt complacency. A famous example of so-called disruptive innovation is the 2014 London Underground strike, which forced local commuters to come up with new ways of getting to and from their jobs. When the strike ended, many of these commuters continued with their altered routines, finding them preferable to riding the underground. Three years after the underground strike, *The Quarterly Journal of Economics* published a case study about it titled "The Benefits of Forced Experimentation," in which the authors concluded that "individuals seem to under-experiment during normal times, as a result of which constraints can be welfare-improving." In other words, people innovate when circumstances change, and "good enough" is no longer good enough.

You might be wondering what all this has to do with endurance sports. The answer is that evolution is not exclusive to biology. Lots of things evolve, including endurance sports. The scientific term for the category of things that evolve is *complex adaptive systems*—a category that encompasses any and all phenomena that consist of heterogenous agents (organisms, athletes) capable of changing (mutating, trying new training methods) in pursuit of success (survival, winning) in a challenging environment (ecosystem, competitions) where success is far from guaranteed. Evolution of some form is certain to happen in a system that meets these criteria. In the natural realm, this process takes the form of amoebas becoming fish becoming lizards becoming dinosaurs becoming birds, and so forth. In endurance sports, it takes the form of improved methods of training, fueling, recovery, etcetera.

Here's the thing: If the principle of good enough applies to the natural realm, it must also apply to other complex adaptive systems, not excepting endurance sports. I used to believe that endurance training methods just kept getting better and better as successive generations of athletes and coaches innovated, relentlessly propelled toward methodological perfection by the pressure of competition. In fact, I still believe this is largely true. But after reading Milo's book, I now recognize that the top athletes of a given generation are under no pressure to discover and practice the most effective training methods possible—they just have to train well enough to win. Sergei Bubka admitted as much, and others have too. John Walker of New Zealand was the first man to run a mile in under 3:50. Later in his career, he told an acquaintance of mine, "Back 1975, when I was 22 years old, if the world record had been 3:47, I would have run 3:46. But the world record was 3:51, so I just ran 3:49."

There are many historical examples of endurance athletes not innovating until they had to. One of these examples is from the 1968 Olympics, which were held in Mexico City, 7,300 feet above sea level. Living at high elevation has always been beneficial to endurance performance. Yet elite athletes made no special effort to claim this advantage until after the Mexico City Games, where Kenya's Kip Keino, who was born and raised at a similar elevation, defeated gold-medal favorite Jim Ryun of the United States in the 1500 meters. Altitude camps have been a staple of elite endurance training ever since.

Overcoming "Good Enough"

A more recent example of disruptive innovation in endurance sports is the advent of carbon-plated super shoes, which were designed to make runners faster in races but have had the greatest impact in training after athletes discovered that running in them left their legs feeling less beat-up, prompting them to experiment with different ways of taking advantage of this unexpected benefit.

The problem with disruptors of this type is that athletes have no control over them. To fend against the inertia of "good enough," athletes must seek out disruptors rather than waiting for them to fall from the sky. Fortunately, there is no shortage of potential disruptors available to athletes at any given time. The most obvious candidates are supplemental and ancillary methods and tools that have scientific backing but, for whatever reason, have not become universal practices among endurance athletes and therefore offer a potential competitive advantage to forward-thinking athletes who take them up.

A case in point is respiratory muscle training (RMT), which entails strengthening the breathing muscles outside the context of full-body exercise. Studies of RMT in athletes have consistently shown it to enhance endurance performance. Despite this, very few athletes—even at the elite level—bother with it, confident that (at least for now) they can win without the hassle of adopting the practice. It's the sports equivalent of the Dvorak keyboard layout: a performance-enhancing alternative to the existing standard that just sits there unused because the existing standard is deemed good enough.

So there's one example of a beneficial potential disruptor that even the pros—who have the most to gain from innovating—are currently passing over. Other supplemental methods are widely practiced by elite athletes but have little uptake among the rest of us. These include glycogen-depleted workouts, which have been shown to increase aerobic capacity not just in elite athletes but in everyday athletes also; hopping exercises, which according to studies improve running economy in athletes of all abilities; and heat training, which increases blood volume, hemoglobin mass, and time-trial performance in temperate environments.

Perhaps you're thinking, *Heck, if a little disruption is good, more must be better!* Why pick one methodological innovation and improve a little when you can pick several and improve a lot? Nice idea, but to get the most benefit from each new practice, you should adopt them individually.

To help you understand why, I will again indulge my penchant for analogy. We've all heard the saying, "A chain is only as strong as its weakest link." But is this really true? If we're talking about an actual physical chain, then yes. Put a chain under sufficient tension and the weakest link will break first, and when a link is broken, the chain is broken. Strengthening the weakest link allows the chain to survive greater tension before a different link—the new weakest—breaks.

It's tempting to assume that an endurance athlete is like a chain. Your performance is limited at any given time by the physiological equivalent of a weak link, which might be anything from low capillary density in the muscles to asymmetries in movement patterns. By adopting a new practice that addresses this weakness, you are able to achieve better performance, but not a lot better because the next weakest link in the physiological chain has become the new limiter. From this perspective, it makes sense to strengthen multiple links simultaneously.

In reality, though, this is not how it works. Endurance performance is not limited by individual physiological weak links. We've seen that respiratory muscle training, glycogen-depleted workouts, hopping exercises, and heat training all enhance endurance performance. Yet each of these methods does so in a different way. If each athlete's performance were limited by a single weak link, only practices that directly affected that limiter would work for any given athlete at any given time. The fact that all of them work tells us that endurance performance is limited not by a single weak link but by how all the links hang together.

Here's a simple way to look at it: At your current level of fitness and development, your body is accustomed to performing at a certain level. Regardless of which new method you adopt or how your body changes in response to it, your entire body has to get used to performing at a new level. Now you see why it's better to adopt new methods one at a time rather than all at once—and also why I refer to such methods as disruptors. When you try three or four new things simultaneously, they count as a single disruption because they're all acting on the same body, which is accustomed to performing at a certain level. But when you try one new thing at a time, waiting for each to achieve its effect before trying another, the next thing acts on a slightly different body, disrupting the new performance paradigm in a way that elevates the athlete to another level of performance.

A good rule of thumb for athletes is to always be trying one new method or tool. To do any less is to allow the good-enough principle to limit your development more than necessary. Any more and you're muting the potential benefit of each innovation by collapsing multiple potential disruptive events into one.

It's also important to be highly selective in choosing new things to try. If elite athletes are often too complacent, innovating no more than necessary to win, others are just the opposite: willing victims of shiny-object syndrome, hopping aboard every new methodological bandwagon that passes by. Don't be that athlete. Evaluate each method critically before adopting it. If science doesn't support it, or if elite athletes don't practice it, then you probably shouldn't practice it either. Use your head. Double threshold workouts *are practiced by elites and do* have scientific support, but they have no place in the training regimen of the majority of athletes who aren't already in the habit of training twice a day.

No athlete is fully impervious to complacency. Not Sergei Bubka, not John Walker, and not you. That's the bad news. The good news is that you don't need to be immune to the good-enough principle to gain a competitive advantage over other athletes with respect to our natural human complacency. You just need to seek out disruptors instead of waiting for them to fall from the sky.

FROM PRINCIPLE TO PRACTICE

Natural complacency causes athletes at all levels, including the very best, to get a little too comfortable with habits that are good enough but could be better, and endurance mastery is achieved by those who actively disrupt their routine in ways calculated to keep them growing. Here are three ideas for turning this principle into practice on your path to mastery:

1/ Take inventory of your current habits and patterns. Where do you see complacency in them? Is there something you keep telling yourself you should be doing that you're still not doing? Perhaps you've been meaning to try the heat-training protocol you learned about a few months ago but you just haven't gotten around to it. Figure out why you haven't yet started and find a way to work around, over, under, or through the barrier. Then do it.

2/ Learn more about new and cutting-edge practices in endurance training. It isn't hard. Just tune out the noise on social media and tune into solid resources like fasttalklabs.com, *The Norwegian Method* by Brad Culp, and Alex Hutchinson's Sweat Science column, where guidance comes from people who get their guidance directly from scientists and elite performers.

3/ Find a club, team, or training group with athletes who are committed to chasing mastery and let their noncomplacency rub off on you, as Mo Farah did by moving in with Craig Mottram (Lesson 2).

Advance in a Different Direction

On November 28, 1950, five months into what would become a four-year war in Korea, United Nations troops under the command of Major General Oliver Smith were surrounded by a vastly larger Chinese force near Chosin Reservoir. Knowing that any attempt to hold their ground would result in annihilation, Smith chose instead to execute a fighting withdrawal, puncturing the Chinese lines on the eastern side and escaping to the Port of Hungnam.

Six days later, Smith found himself standing before a gaggle of American war correspondents who'd been flown in by the military for an update on the conflict. Pressed to explain his retreat, he snapped angrily, "Retreat, hell! We're not retreating, we're just advancing in a different direction." Smith couldn't possibly have known at the time that these words would immortalize him, surviving his death on Christmas Day 1977 and living on today as the primary association with his name. (Google "Major General Oliver Smith" if you don't believe me.) The quote appeared in the lead paragraph of an article in the December 18, 1950, issue of *Time* magazine, under the headline, "War: Retreat of the 20,000." Ridiculed as mendacious at best, and delusional at worst, Smith's utterance has been cited ever since as a classic example of military doublespeak, right up there with, "We had to burn the village to save the village."

After the war, Smith defended his choice of language as tactically accurate. "You can't retreat or withdraw when you are surrounded," he explained to one historian. "The only thing you can do is break out. When you break out, you attack. That's what we were doing." My own interest in Smith's infamous line is less historical than psychological. While its tactical accuracy can be debated, what is certain is that, in referring to the actions of his troops at Chosin Reservoir as "advancing in a different direction," Smith was making an overt effort to put a positive spin on a negative situation. Psychologists call this mental trick *cognitive reframing*, and it's very useful to endurance athletes and coaches.

The technique originated with Albert Ellis, best remembered as the father of cognitive behavioral therapy (CBT). Born in 1913 and raised in the Bronx, Ellis got early exposure to caregiving after his father abandoned him with two younger siblings and a mentally ill mother. He later studied psychology at City College, where he learned the tenets and practices of psychoanalysis, but his subsequent clinical work led him to become disillusioned with the Freudian paradigm, and he eventually put forward an evidence-based alternative now known as CBT, which remains the most widely practiced psychotherapeutic method.

As the name implies, cognitive behavioral therapy seeks to change a person's thoughts and behaviors insofar as they are deemed problematic. The technique of cognitive reframing is used specifically to replace unhelpful thoughts with helpful thoughts. This might sound like an invitation to wishful thinking, but a thought isn't really helpful if it isn't grounded in reality. Cognitive reframing is not about replacing unpleasant realities with pleasant illusions; it's about shifting your perspective on reality in ways that solve problems. Oliver Smith did not pretend that his troops hadn't been surrounded by a vastly larger Chinese force at Chosin Reservoir or wish that a miracle would save them. He simply made a decision to execute a fighting withdrawal and reframed it as an advance rather than a retreat—a perspective shift that undoubtedly benefited the morale of the men doing the fighting.

A good way to get started with cognitive reframing is the "yes, but" exercise. Whenever you experience a negative thought about a situation, acknowledge its veracity with a "yes," then quickly add a truthful "but" statement that is more helpful. For example, if the negative thought is, *That workout went rather poorly*, you might say to yourself, *Yes, but I did the work and I will benefit from it just as much as I would have if the workout had gone spectacularly.*

Cognitive Reframing

The full version of cognitive reframing consists of five steps. Let's see how they apply to a hypothetical situation where you're worried that you don't have enough time to get fully ready for an upcoming race. How might you reframe this situation to get the best possible outcome?

STEP 1: DEFINE THE PROBLEM.

Problems are almost always signaled by negative emotions. Too often, we focus not on the problem itself but on the emotion that comes with it, and when we do, the inevitable outcome is unskillful management of the problem. This first step in the process of cognitive reframing forces us to separate the problem from the emotion and look at it objectively, setting ourselves up to address the problem instead of taking our eyes off the ball in an effort to make the emotion go away.

The problem in this case is that you might not have enough time to get fully ready for the race (*obviously*), and worry is the emotion attached to it. Many athletes in this situation will fixate on their worry, looking outside themselves for soothing as a child would, except instead of asking their daddy to hold them, they ask their coach to assure them there is enough time. There's a scared child in all of us, but as adult athletes, we're better off defining our problems objectively, thereby distancing them from the emotion that brought them to our attention. In the hypothetical case before us, you might enact step one of cognitive reframing by sitting down with your journal and writing the following words: "I might not have enough time to get fully ready for my upcoming race." Words a robot would say (if robots ran marathons).

STEP 2: IDENTIFY HOW THE PROBLEM MAKES YOU FEEL.

It's one thing to feel a certain way, another thing to reflect on how you're feeling. When you feel a certain way without reflecting on it, the feeling controls you. But when you step back and consider your feelings, you have the power to control them. In the example before us, if you feel worried without reflecting on this emotion, you're likely to make worry-driven decisions and fail to recognize other options for addressing the problem. Labeling the emotion after defining the problem underscores the separateness of these two things, enabling you to address each element individually through appropriate measures.

STEP 3: EXPLAIN THE PROBLEM.

Step three entails explaining to yourself *why* the problem is a problem, or in what ways you are or might be harmed by the situation. In the case of doubting you have enough time to get fully ready for an upcoming race, your explanation might look something like this: "If

I'm not fully ready for the race when the day arrives, I will perform below my expectations, and if I perform below my expectations, I will feel disappointed."

STEP 4: EXAMINE THE PROBLEM.

Having defined the problem, identified how it makes you feel, and explained the harm the problem is causing or may cause, you're in a position to assess whether you have any choice in these matters. Is the problem you've defined actually the true problem, or even a problem at all? Do you have to feel the way you feel about it? How harmful is the harm, really? It's possible that you have in fact defined the problem correctly, that you can't easily change how you feel about it, and that the harm you perceive is real and unexaggerated. But in many cases, examining the problem before you with a critical eye leads you to recognize that you do have choices.

The American Psychological Association offers the following nine questions as prompts for step four of cognitive reframing:

1/ Is there another way of looking at the situation?

2/ Is there an alternative explanation for what happened?

3/ How would someone else think about the situation?

4/ Is my concern based more on how I feel than the actual facts in the situation?

5/ Am I placing unrealistic and unobtainable standards on myself that I would never expect other people to achieve?

6/ Am I overestimating how much control and responsibility I have in this situation?

7/ What would be the worst thing that could happen if my fear were true?

8/ Am I not considering everything I can do to deal with the problem or situation?

9 / Am I thinking that because a low-probability event happened to me, that it is very likely to happen again to me?

Not all of these questions are relevant to the problem of doubting you have enough time to get fully ready for an upcoming race, or to any other problem, but they faithfully represent the spirit of this step in the process of cognitive reframing. The questions I might ask you in this particular situation if I were your coach are number one, number three, and number seven.

Is there another way of looking at the situation? Of course! If you're fairly certain you will not be fully ready for your race, you can skip it and find another race to do. But if you prefer to take your chances on the race you're currently targeting, you can at least recognize this choice as a choice and not something that is being forced on you.

How would someone else look at this situation? It so happens that I myself am currently preparing for a race that I don't think I will be fully ready for, and I'm not worried about it. So it's clearly not necessary to be worried in this type of situation or to view it as a problem. What is different about athletes who feel little or no worry when they doubt they have enough time to get fully ready for an upcoming race? One possibility is that they don't care how they perform. A more likely possibility is that they are comfortable with the uncertainty of the situation. To me, this insight gets to the heart of the issue.

When an athlete of mine expresses worry in the face of uncertainty about how things will turn out, I ask them if they watch sports. Having received an affirmative answer, I ask them if they would still watch sports if they knew in advance how every game would turn out. Having received a negative answer, I ask them if the uncertainty of outcomes is what makes watching sports exciting. Having received an affirmative answer, I ask them why participating in sports should be any different. Worry is a natural response to uncertainty in the athletic experience, but it's not the only possible response. Excitement—a form of curiosity—is another. Uncertainty can never be completely eliminated from the process, which means it must be dealt with. Athletes who embrace it with a spirit of curious excitement not only have a more pleasant experience but also tend to achieve better outcomes, because worry is a performance killer.

What would be the worst thing that could happen if my fear were true? We've answered this one already. The worst thing that could happen if you're not fully ready come race day is that you perform below expectations and feel disappointed. That's not exactly the end of the world, is it? Nor is it an automatic response to underperforming. Endurance masters judge their performances not by final outcomes but by how well they execute. We saw this with Dave Scott, who won the Ironman World Championship six times but rated a fifth-place finish in 1996 as his best race. You can and should feel great about any race you execute brilliantly, even when the outcome is below expectations due to lack of fitness, setbacks in training, inclement weather, or any other factor that is outside your control.

STEP 5: MAKE A DECISION.

The fifth and final step in the process of cognitive reframing is to decide whether to change your perspective on the problem. Returning once more to our hypothetical example, you must decide what to do about the fact that you might not have enough time to get fully ready for your upcoming race. There are three options, one of which—skipping the race and finding a later one to do instead—has already been mentioned. Another option is to stay your present course, hoping you actually do have enough time, worrying you don't, and seeking assurance wherever you can find it. The third option is to accept that you simply don't know how things will turn out and embrace the challenge of controlling what you can to run a race you're proud of.

The first option is perfectly valid, but it's not an example of cognitive reframing. I've often endorsed athletes' decisions to skip races they don't feel ready for and try again at a later date. But while this is a viable solution in some cases, every athlete must sooner or later deal with uncertainty instead of eliminating it. And in this case, the better way to deal with uncertainty is to reframe the situation as an exciting challenge.

Always Advancing

My favorite example of cognitive reframing is the one we started with: Major General Oliver Smith's immortal phrase, "advancing in a different direction." For those who've mastered the art of finding the most helpful perspective on the challenges they encounter, there is always a legitimate sense in which they are moving forward, even when it looks like retreat to outsiders.

Most athletes don't think this way. They distinguish between periods of moving forward and periods when they are stuck in place or going backward. When they are healthy and getting fitter and things are going their way, they are moving forward, and when they are hurt or losing fitness or things aren't going their way, they are moving backward. Endurance mastery requires that you identify a path forward in every situation. A disappointing race is a powerful motivator that might lift you to new heights of performance the next time around. An injury is an opportunity to learn how to avoid future injuries. A cosmic fireball colliding with planet Earth and wiping out humanity is—well, okay, there's a limit.

FROM PRINCIPLE TO PRACTICE

Athletes have the freedom to adopt different perspectives on the challenges they encounter, and endurance mastery relies on consistently finding the most helpful perspective. Here are three ideas for turning this principle into practice on your path to mastery:

1/ Identify the biggest sport-related problem you face currently and reframe it. For me it's long COVID, a form of chronic fatigue I've carried for several years, and I've reframed it as a challenge to come up with my own playbook for a situation that has no standard playbook. Now you try.

2/ Get in the habit of flagging any negative emotions you experience as an athlete. Remember, negative emotions signal problems, and the sooner you become aware of a problem, the sooner you can start the process of finding the most helpful perspective on it. In my case, frustration most often signals the need to find a more helpful perspective on my health.

3/ Use cognitive reframing with problems you encounter outside of sports, such as relationship friction, money worries, and work stress. The extra practice will accelerate your mastery of the method, benefiting your problem-solving efforts in life and sport.

Train in Style

Frank Shorter made his mark as a marathoner. Yet he trained like a 5000-meter runner, grinding out blistering interval sets on the track twice a week. It must have worked, because he won a gold medal at the 1972 Olympics.

Joan Benoit Samuelson seldom planned her workouts in advance, preferring instead to go by feel most days. Her "seat of the pants" training style, as she once described it to me, stood in stark contrast to the structured approach favored by most professional runners, but it, too, must have worked, because Samuelson won a gold medal at the 1984 Olympics.

Steve Jones ran significantly less than his elite peers—just 70 miles per week on average—but kept the pace high the majority of the time. Again, it must have worked, because he set a world record for the marathon in 1984.

Constantina Dita trained with mind-numbing monotony, repeating the same few runs week in and week out. Her victory in the 2008 Olympic Marathon suggests this also worked.

More recently, Spanish mountain runner Kilian Jornet perfected a personal training style that's as eclectic as Constantina Dita's was repetitious, combining daily running in wide-ranging environments with cycling, ski mountaineering, and alpine climbing. It appears this unorthodox hodgepodge works for Jornet, who has won most of the world's biggest ultramarathons, including the Western States 100 and Ultra-Trail du Mont-Blanc.

Cam Levins runs quite a bit more than the typical elite marathoner—170 miles per week, and often three times a day. Look no further than his 2:05:36 clocking at the 2023 Tokyo Marathon (the fastest marathon ever run by a North American) for proof that Levins's unusual way of training works as well for him as the other approaches I've described worked for those who created them.

I could keep going, but you get the idea. What these examples illustrate is that there are many different ways to train effectively as an endurance athlete. But what does this mean exactly? On the one hand, it could mean that the most effective way to train is slightly different for each athlete. On the other hand, it might indicate that any given athlete is capable of performing equally well with a variety of different training programs. Suppose Joan Benoit Samuelson had followed Constantina Dita's unvarying routine. Would she still have won the 1984 Olympic Marathon? Would Cam Levins still be running 2:05 marathons if he switched to Steve Jones's low-mileage regimen?

To the best of my knowledge, no one has ever asked Frank Shorter if he could have thrived on Killian Jornet's potpourri methodology, nor has anyone invited Jornet to speculate on whether he would win as often as he does if he switched to Shorter's track-focused system. Yet I'm confident that if such questions were put forward, the answer in all cases would be an emphatic no. I say this because each of the athletes in the foregoing litany has, at one time or another, publicly credited their distinctive way of training for their success. To doubt these judgments from the proverbial horses' mouths would be the height of disrespect. So we're left to conclude that, although there is more than one way to train effectively as an endurance athlete, not all athletes can achieve the same level of success with just any training method chosen from among the many that have brought success to certain individuals. The variety we see in elite training styles comes less from the fact that there is more than one way to skin a cat in endurance training than from the fact that each athlete has an optimal way of training that is different from other athletes' ideal recipes.

The obvious explanation for the variety of individual training styles seen at the elite level is genetic diversity, and indeed, science offers strong support for this idea. In 2020, researchers studied the effects of different endurance training methods on recreational runners. The subjects spent three weeks practicing each of three training regimens—high intensity, high volume, and high frequency—in random order. All of the runners improved by varying amounts with the three training regimens, but there was no clear winner. Some improved the most on high-volume training, others got more benefit from high-intensity training, and still other responded best to high-frequency training, leading the study's authors to conclude, "Pronounced differences in individual physiological adaptation may occur following various training mesocycles in runners."

It should be noted that this study has clear limitations, including the small number of participants (13), the brevity of their exposure to each regimen, and their lack of correspondence with how athletes actually train in the real world. But the biggest limitation, as it relates to our discussion, is that the runners did not get to choose their own training program, and the experiment therefore tells us nothing about how the most successful athletes end up with their unique methodologies. But who needs a study when the answer to this mystery has already been given by the athletes themselves?

Personality and Preferences

In interviews, biographies, and elsewhere, top athletes with quirky training styles have all explained why they train as they do, and physiology per se has little bearing on it. Elite athletes don't enter an exercise lab and test various approaches under expert supervision before committing to the one that yields the greatest amount of measured improvement. Instead, in almost every case, they follow their preferences. Why did Joan Benoit Samuelson train by the seat of her pants rather than planning her workouts in advance? Because she felt like it. Why did Steve Jones choose not to run as much as his fellow elite marathoners? Because he didn't want to.

Let's talk about mice for a moment. As with humans, some mice enjoy running more than others. If you put a dozen mice in a dozen cages, each with a running wheel, some will spend a lot of time on that wheel, others almost none, and the rest will fall somewhere in the middle. Scientists have completed dozens of experiments in the hope of learning what's different about mice that love to run, including some in which exercise-loving mice were selectively bred and then dissected to see how their physiology changed across generations as their running penchant intensified. The first place they looked for such changes was in the muscles, where they expected to discover evidence that the more structurally suited a mouse was to running (stronger heart, faster legs), the more time they chose to spend running. For the most part, though, these efforts came up empty, and what was discovered instead was that the most important changes happened in the brain. Each generation of selectively bred mice ran more than the previous one not because they had developed running bodies but because, in essence, they had developed *running personalities*.

I believe it's the same with Constantina Dita and Kilian Jornet and other elite endurance athletes who fall outside the mainstream in one way or another in their approach to training. They train the way they do because they enjoy it, and because they enjoy it, it's effective. No doubt there's some overlap between physiology and psychology. Cam Levins likes running a lot, but it's evident that the 50 extra miles per week he's running compared to the typical elite runner are making him fitter, whereas they would cause most others to break down. It makes intuitive sense that what's good for an athlete training-wise *feels* good to them, and what isn't doesn't, and here again science affirms our intuition.

Gareth Sandford is a Canada-based British exercise physiologist whose work focuses on identifying physiological differences between individual endurance athletes and figuring out how to customize their training in ways that yield the most benefit. Sanford's favorite tests for getting an initial read on a person's physiology are a 10-second sprint to assesses raw power; a 6-minute time trial assessing aerobic capacity; and a 20-minute time trial, which gauges threshold fitness. As an alternative to these tests, Sandford simply asks athletes to name their favorite and least favorite workouts. Almost invariably, he told me, athletes prefer workouts that suit their physiology and dislike workouts that challenge their weaknesses.

Additional evidence of overlapping physiology and psychology in personal training styles comes from a 2024 study appearing in *PLOS One*. An international team of researchers led by Frenchman Cyrille Gindre measured personality characteristics and running biomechanics in a group of 80 adults. They found that runners classified as *sensers* (because they allow their senses to inform their behavior) ran differently than runners classified as *intuitives* (because they prefer a top-down approach to regulating their behavior) in mathematically precise ways. We all know that the actual structure of our bodies plays a big role in how our bodies move. But it appears our personalities also play a big role in how our bodies move, and if this is true, it stands to reason that our personalities influence how we choose to train as well.

We've seen already that, for purely physical reasons, athletes should approach the training process as an open experiment, identifying patterns of cause and effect and retaining practices that seem to yield good results while discarding those that don't. What I'm now suggesting is that you do something similar on a psychological level, allowing your preferences to shape your training into a signature style. To the extent that psychological preferences overlap with physiological effectiveness, indulging your partialities in this manner will lead to more or less the same results as studying quantitative cause and effect.

Certain training preferences have more to do with personality than with physiology. Take Frank Shorter, the guy who trained like a 5K runner even though he was primarily a marathoner. It so happens that Frank was horrifically abused as a boy by his father, an experience that left him with an exceptional capacity to cope with pain. The searing high-intensity track workouts he did twice a week were his way of indulging and honing this special gift, and had little to do with his physical makeup. Examples like this one teach us that each athlete has a personal optimal training *style* that is somewhat distinct from their personal optimal training *formula*, the former being psychologically defined and the latter being physiologically determined. It's important that you give equal attention to both cause-and-effect patterns and individual tastes in searching for a unified training style/formula.

Taking a cue from the pros, I go out of my way to indulge the training preferences of the athletes I coach. I've got one runner who grew up as a swimmer and still loves the water. So, twice a week I have her run in the pool instead of on land. Another athlete likes to go on periodic multiday mountain treks, so I came up with a way to fit them into his training. A third client gets bored easily, so I devise all kinds of novel workouts for her, some of which are downright peculiar in format. I'm certain that all of these athletes are getting better results than they would if we did everything completely by the book, ignoring the mind and focusing exclusively on the body.

I recognize that allowing personal preferences to guide your approach to training is not without risks. A less experienced or knowledgeable runner who enjoys CrossFit, for example, might lace their training with too much CrossFit, the optimal amount of which is zero. Or a lazy runner who hates long runs because they happen to target their greatest weakness might eschew them, putting all their energy into strengthening their strengths, a losing strategy for those who claim to want to reach their full potential.

Like most of the things that skillful self-regulators do and other athletes don't, developing a personal training style isn't easy. It requires self-awareness, self-trust, and a degree of creativity: self-awareness to identify your likes and dislikes, self-trust to defy conventional practices in favor of these preferences, and creativity to develop an overall style of training that combines idiosyncrasy and conventionality in a way that works. There's no getting around the fact that these requirements for developing a personal training style place a burden of responsibility on the individual athlete and their coach that simply cannot be foisted upon anyone else, much less a piece of technology.

On the plus side is the fact that with this responsibility comes a certain freedom. It is an unquestionable fact that if you allow your preferences to shape your training style—either with or without the help of a coach—you are more likely to reach your full potential. That's pretty neat!

FROM PRINCIPLE TO PRACTICE

Developing a personal training style that fits your personality and preferences is essential to your pursuit of mastery. Here are three ideas for turning this principle into practice:

1/ Take a personality test. There are many options, but I prefer the athlete-specific Sports Personality Questionnaire, which is available at myskillsprofile.com for a modest cost. The insights you gain from undergoing a formal personality assessment will help you start to shape your optimal training style.

2/ Open up your journal and take a few minutes to describe your current style of training. Focus on defining characteristics (e.g., "lots of trail running") and aspects that are different from how most of your peers train (e.g., "high-intensity training done almost entirely on hills"). Consider your reasons for training the way you do and whether there is room to modify your training to better match your motivational profile.

3/ Try something different that appeals to your personality and preferences and is outside the norms of endurance training yet carries a plausible benefit. For example, if you're a creative person you might give yourself permission to invent your own workouts. If you're on the compulsive side, consider starting a run streak. Think outside the box and experiment, retaining the thing you try if it yields good results and discarding it if it doesn't.

Be a Fox

A thletes who consistently make good decisions reach their full potential. Athletes who fail to make good decisions consistently fall short of their potential. It's as simple as that. But what does it take to make good decisions? At the most basic level, a good decision has two requirements: information and judgment. Of these, judgment is by far the more important in most contexts, including the ones in which endurance athletes and coaches make their decisions.

Information is overvalued, quite frankly. This was shown in a study appearing in *Medicine & Science in Sports & Exercise* in 2017. Two groups of cyclists—one novice, the other experienced—were given access to six different types of data—speed, distance, power output, heart rate, cadence, and time—while performing simulated 10-mile time trials. Special sensors were used to track the cyclists' eye movements in order to determine which data sources they were attending to while they pedaled. To the surprise of no one, the experienced cyclists performed significantly better than the novices. But they also processed information differently, focusing mainly on speed and tuning out less relevant data, such as cadence, while the novices' eyes were all over the place, leading the authors of the study to conclude that experienced cyclists "are more selective and consistent in attention to feedback during [time-trial] cycling."

We can infer from these results that athletes learn through experience to be selective in their information inputs when making pacing decisions. With practice, each athlete develops a robust internal sense of pacing that requires minimal information input to generate reliable decisions about how hard to push at any given moment. Whereas novices are utterly dependent on information to make such decisions, veterans rely on judgment, using it skillfully to filter and contextualize information inputs.

Experience doesn't improve judgment or reduce information dependence equally in everyone, however. Independent of experience, some people naturally prefer to lean on information when making decisions, while others rely more on judgment. Philosopher Isaiah Berlin labeled the first type *hedgehogs* (a burrowing animal that is said to know a lot about a little) and the second type *foxes* (a scanning animal that knows a little about a lot). While Berlin used the terms half-jokingly, science writer David Epstein takes them quite seriously in his bestselling 2019 book *Range*, where he notes that hedgehogs tend to perform better in what psychologist Daniel Kahneman calls "kind" learning environments, in which "a learner improves simply by engaging in the activity and trying to do better," while foxes excel in "wicked" learning environments, where "the rules of the game are often unclear or incomplete, there may or may not be repetitive patterns and they may not be obvious, and the feedback is often delayed, inaccurate, or both." An example of a kind learning environment is chess, a game that, although difficult to master, is far neater and tidier than real-life challenges like managing a business, which is an example of a wicked learning environment.

Evidence that possessing a little information and a lot of judgment (as foxes prefer) is better than having a lot of information and a little judgment (as hedgehogs prefer) in most real-world situations comes from a famous prediction tournament, described in Epstein's book, that was organized by the Intelligence Advanced Research Projects Activity (IARPA). Teams of forecasters were asked to bet on the likelihood of certain geopolitical events occurring at specific future times. Most of the teams were made up of highly specialized military intelligence experts, who collectively got their asses handed to them by a team called the Good Judgment Project, which was made up of nonexperts who were selected specifically for their foxlike thinking skills rather than their knowledge, and who outperformed the well-informed experts by an estimated 30 percent.

The problem that hedgehogs face in wicked learning environments is that they can't tolerate ambiguity or uncertainty, so they pretend it doesn't exist. Entirely reliant on the single tool of gathering information to fill the void of uncertainty, they make decisions based upon the data they have and simply ignore the information gaps. My name for this tendency is the *illusion of completeness*. Foxes, meanwhile, operate as creative problem solvers. They like information, but they use their judgment to filter and contextualize the information they possess instead of allowing it to be the sole determinant of their decisions, regardless of its incompleteness.

"Beneath complexity," Epstein writes, "hedgehogs tend to see simple, deterministic rules of cause and effect framed by their area of expertise, like repeating patterns on a chessboard. Foxes see complexity in what others mistake for simple cause and effect. They understand that most cause-and-effect relationships are probabilistic, not deterministic. There are unknowns, and luck, and even when history repeats, it does not do so precisely."

Here's the $64,000 question: *Is endurance sport a kind learning environment, like the game of chess, or a wicked learning environment, like managing a business?* In other words, is the overall context in which endurance athletes pursue greater performance tidy enough and stable enough that information matters more than judgment, or is it sufficiently messy and uncertain that judgment matters more than information in making decisions? Athletes, coaches, and sports scientists with hedgehog minds want to believe endurance sport is a kind learning environment. They tell themselves that by paying very close attention to data from power meters, heart rate monitors, and other devices, they can make the right decisions reliably without reference to any bigger picture.

An example of this type is former University of Oregon track and field coach Robert Johnson, who once said, "Track is nothing but numbers. A good mathematician probably could be a good track coach." The problem with this statement is that Johnson himself was not a good track coach *because he treated athletes as numbers.* The quote I just shared was given to a reporter for *The Oregonian* newspaper after several of Johnson's former athletes publicly accused him of causing eating disorders by subjecting them to frequent weigh-ins and DEXA scans, all in the name of controlling the numbers. In response to these allegations, three separate investigations into Johnson's conduct were launched, and in the end, he lost his job.

The correct answer to the question I asked a minute ago (contrary to what you'll hear from the likes of Robert Johnson) is *B, wicked.* The developmental process in endurance sports is extremely complex, and any attempt to reduce it to numbers is misbegotten and doomed to fail. This doesn't mean hedgehogs can't be successful as coaches and athletes, but what it does mean is that to have any hope of being as successful as those with foxy tendencies, hedgehogs must discover their inner fox.

Which is easier said than done, I'm afraid. Hedgehog brains are wired to fear uncertainty and ambiguity and to eliminate it through the lone instrument of information gathering. But here's the good news: Research has shown that foxlike thinking is trainable to some degree, and that individuals who receive this training make better decisions subsequently.

One tool that both coaches and athletes can use to become more foxlike in their thinking is what's known as the *recognition heuristic*. When confronted with a problem that lacks an immediate and obvious answer, ask yourself, *Does anything about this situation remind me of something I've encountered previously?* Unlike hedgehogs, who struggle to see beneath the surface of data, foxes are able, in Epstein's words, to "probe for deep structural similarities to the current problem in different ones" by applying "flexible mental schemes." The recognition heuristic can help you frame information within a bigger picture, as foxes do.

A Fox in Action

I thought it might be helpful to conclude this lesson with a true story of a fox in action, a role model for other coaches and athletes, who operates as a creative problem solver and takes a judgment-led, information-guided approach to decision-making.

The story begins in September 2018, when Angelina Ramos was in her first year of coaching track and field at the University of Nevada Las Vegas and Agnes Mansaray was a newly arrived and highly touted transfer from Iowa Central Community College (by way of her native Sierra Leone), where she had been a dominant force in cross-country and track. It didn't take long for Ramos to see why. Mansaray crushed every workout her new coach threw at her, bolstering the team's prospects for the season ahead.

Then it all went kerflooey. Midway through the fall cross-country season, Mansaray developed a pain in her lower back. Mild at first, the pain grew steadily worse, to the point that it literally stopped her in her tracks some days. Yet she continued to train and race, even when the discomfort spread to her head, multiplying her woes with thunderous migraines. The inevitable crisis came at the Mountain West Conference Championships in San Diego, where Mansaray collapsed just 800 meters into the 6,000-meter race, clutching her back and howling piteously, and was rushed to the hospital.

Like any good coach—fox or hedgehog—Ramos wanted information. Given the nature of Mansaray's problem, much of this information would necessarily come from doctors, but it took many weeks to get a clear diagnosis (namely, tumors growing on and around her kidney), and in the meantime Ramos took it upon herself to do her own research and test hunches. A hedgehog in Ramos's place would have gone no further than gathering information to fill the vacuum surrounding her athlete's mystery ailment and basing their decisions entirely on this information. But Ramos is a fox, so she went much further, accepting the uncertainty of the situation and using her judgment to be the best coach she could be despite the wickedness of the environment.

Judging that Mansaray needed to feel cared for, Ramos accompanied her to every doctor's appointment and hospital visit and helped her navigate the byzantine American healthcare system. There was no data to support these caring efforts, but they helped.

Judging that Mansaray would benefit psychologically from being actively involved in the search for a fix, Ramos took her to see a shaman after learning that her family back home in Sierra Leone believed a jealous enemy had placed a curse upon her. There was no data to support this effort at empowerment, but Ramos didn't care. "At the end of the day, it doesn't matter what the coach believes," she told me.

Judging that Mansaray needed hope more than anything, Ramos gave her something to hold on to every day. At one of her lowest moments, as Mansaray lay recovering in a hospital bed, Ramos vowed to her, "I will put you on the podium at Conference," referring to the Mountain West Conference Indoor Track and Field Championships. There sure as heck wasn't any data to support this promise, but it had the desired effect nonetheless, giving Mansaray a measure of hope.

Just seven weeks before the big meet, Mansaray was cleared to resume running. Judging that she needed confidence as much as she needed fitness, Ramos shaped her training to this purpose, shifting her from distance-based runs to time-based runs so she wouldn't compare her current self to her past self, and having her do workouts apart from the team so she wouldn't compare herself to her fitter teammates. In the one opportunity Mansaray got to compete before the conference meet, Ramos kept her out of the A heat of the 800 meters, where she normally belonged, and placed her in the B heat, which she won, bolstering her confidence. Two weeks later, Mansaray broke the Sierra Leonean national record for her event, her time of 2:08.31 earning her a second-place finish in the conference and fulfilling her coach's hospital-room promise.

How to Be Extra

Toward the end of her tumor ordeal, when things were looking a little brighter, Mansaray asked Ramos, "Coach, why are you so extra?" I should note that English is Mansaray's fourth language, so she doesn't always have the right word to express a thought or feeling, but I think we all know what she meant in this instance. Angelina Ramos had gone the extra mile in coaching Agnes Mansaray through her struggle, and Mansaray appreciated it. Quite a contrast to how hedgehog Robert Johnson's athletes felt about him!

You are not a number, and like all athletes, you are more than the sum of your inner workings. Numbers and physiology are important, but information alone will not suffice to support good coaching decisions. The most successful athletes operate as creative problem solvers, using information selectively and contextually to inform their judgment. They accept the reality that an element of uncertainty exists in every situation requiring a decision, and they understand that more data won't relieve them of the responsibility to exercise good judgment.

There are problems athletes encounter for which there is no established playbook, and there are athletes who, in one way or another, are exceptions to the norm. If you find yourself in a position to choose a coach, choose one who doesn't wait for extreme cases like Agnes Mansaray's to do and be "extra." Choose a fox like Angelina Ramos who writes their own playbook with each athlete and sees the exceptional in everyone.

You really are one of a kind, as is every new challenge you encounter. Seldom will you truly *know* what to do when faced with a tough decision. But you can make the right decision more often than not by leaning on judgment more than you do on information.

Another interesting fact about foxes and hedgehogs is that foxes are fast, and hedgehogs are slow.

FROM PRINCIPLE TO PRACTICE

You must make good decisions consistently to reach your full potential, and doing so requires a "fox" mindset, where judgment plays a bigger role than information. Here are three ideas for turning this principle into practice on your path to mastery:

1/ Take stock of your current approach to making decisions. Do device data and other information guide your decisions or control them? How comfortable are you making decisions in situations of uncertainty? Take these reflections into your next decision and try a more foxlike approach, focusing on the most relevant information, placing it in context, recognizing the unknown elements of the situation, and trusting your judgment.

2/ Assess the outcome of your most recent decision. How did it work out? What can you learn from the experience? Apply the lesson to your next decision, aiming again to think like a fox, but more effectively this time.

3/ Get in the habit of "zooming out" mentally to see the bigger picture whenever you confront a challenge that requires a decision from you. High-level construal comes easily to some athletes and not so easily to others. Instead of just labeling the problem in a reactive way (e.g., "hip pain"), contextualize it. Is the problem truly isolated, or is it part of a broader pattern? Is the problem novel, or have you experienced things like it before, and if so, what did you learn from those prior incidents? Did the problem strike out of nowhere, or were there indications that it was coming? Have things been going well for you aside from this problem, or is it a small part of a bigger off-track period in your training? Asking yourself these types of questions will help you make more foxlike decisions.

CHALLENGE

How to Push Your Limits

———

The fifth and final pillar of endurance mastery invites you to seek new and greater challenges for the purpose of expanding your capacity to control your emotions, thoughts, and actions in pursuit of your goals.

In this section you will explore these five lessons and how they might open up new ways to challenge yourself:

21

Overcoming your natural human tendency
toward self-deception is essential to achieving mastery.

22

Restraint is at least as important as grit
with respect to fulfilling your potential.

23

It is beneficial to approach your sport as a vehicle
for becoming the best version of yourself.

24

To find the absolute limit of your ability,
you must value challenges more than performance.

25

Constraints—including the constraint of aging—
present opportunities to improve, provided you embrace them as such.

Keep It Real

On a Monday afternoon in the spring of 1987 I found myself standing at a urinal in a boys' bathroom located just outside the gymnasium at Oyster River High School in Durham, New Hampshire, where I was a sophomore member of the outdoor track and field team. To my immediate right, engaged in the same bodily function, was Jeff Johnson, who coached our girls' team, but is best known as Nike's first employee and the man who gave the company its name.

"Was that a PR for you?" Johnson asked, keeping his eyes forward.

He was referring to a mile race I'd won two days earlier with a time of 4:44, which was indeed a personal best.

"Yeah, but it was a tactical race," I lied, adopting the blasé adolescent tone that adults find so annoying. "The time doesn't mean much."

In truth, the race had been a street fight, a wildly nontactical struggle that featured four lead changes and took everything I had to emerge from as the victor.

"Really?" Johnson said. "It looked like a street fight to me."

Robbed of my tongue, I quickly flushed, zipped, and fled the bathroom. Johnson had called bullshit on me, plain and simple, and I had no defense. Yet despite my embarrassment, I felt great respect for him in that moment. He was an exceptional coach, having transformed our girls' cross-country team from a one-member cellar-dweller into state champions in the span of three years. Anyone else would have stayed mum in the situation I just described, allowing my self-deception to go unchallenged. But exceptional coaches keep it real with athletes, never abetting the lies they so often tell themselves.

"In our program, the truth is the basis of all that we do," said the legendary Duke University men's basketball coach Mike Krzyzewski. "There is nothing more important than the truth because there's nothing more powerful than the truth. Consequently, on our team, we always tell one another the truth. We must be honest with one another. There is no other way."

As a coach now myself, I maintain the same insistence on truthfulness that Jeff Johnson and Mike Krzyzewski did with their athletes. I'll give you an example. It concerns a runner we'll call Alan, who came to me with a set of ambitious time goals that, for him, represented the standard for qualifying as a "real runner." He was determined to hit these marks, which I had no problem with in principle, but in Alan's case, fixating on certain numbers caused him to get ahead of himself. I'd give him pace targets based on his current fitness level and he'd disregard them, starting off at the pace he wanted to run, then blowing up and struggling to finish. The first time it happened, I gently admonished Alan, explaining why his overaggressive pacing did not serve his interests and extracting from him a promise not to repeat the error. But repeat it he did, not once but multiple times, offering a new rationalization for his noncompliance in each instance.

Things came to a head when I gave Alan a set of 600-meter intervals at 5K race pace. Once again, he started too fast and had to dig deep to hang on. Afterward, when I demanded an explanation, Alan told me that the pace he'd run had truly felt sustainable for 5K in race conditions. At my wit's end, I called his bluff, replacing Alan's next workout with a simple challenge: prove to me that you really can hold that pace for 5K. He made it just over a mile.

My goal was not to punish Alan but to jolt him out of the rut of self-deception he was stuck in. The next time we spoke, he confessed that he just couldn't accept where he was in his running—that the whole process felt like a waste if he wasn't able to hit the times a "real runner" could run. We parted ways shortly thereafter.

I don't consider this a bad outcome. A coach must be unbending in their defense of reality against an athlete's self-deceptions. If the athlete believes some wacko UFO conspiracy theory, that's none of the coach's business. But when a self-deception impedes an athlete's progress toward fulfilling their potential, the coach has a duty to address it. I feel better about losing Alan as a client than I would have felt about not doing what I had to do to pierce the illusion he'd created and allow him to make a clear-eyed choice about what he really wanted.

All of us are prone to self-deception. In a 2011 paper titled "Evolution and the Psychology of Self-Deception," psychologist William von Hippel and anthropologist Robert Trivers argue that, although many animal species evolved the capacity to deceive other organisms in the war for survival, humans alone developed the additional capacity to deceive *themselves* as an aid to outward deception. When we believe the deceptions we perpetrate against others, von Hippel and Trivers explain, we are less likely to exhibit behavioral cues associated with deception (or "tells," as poker players call them).

This doesn't mean that self-deception is always useful, however, and in the context of sports it's seldom useful. It's easy to see why. To solve real problems, athletes must see reality clearly. Alan was never going to become the runner he wanted to be by *pretending* he was that runner already. He needed to accept where he was and take things one step at a time. What kept him from doing so was fear—specifically, fear of not measuring up to a certain standard.

Even the greatest athletes experience fear. The difference is that, when they do, they usually find their own way through the self-deceptions that are engendered by this emotion. One such athlete is Daniela Ryf of Switzerland, winner of ten triathlon world championship titles at the Ironman and Ironman 70.3 distances. Ryf's dominance created an aura of invincibility that she recognized as an advantage, but it came at a cost. "I realized that fooling others, and especially myself, was bad for my well-being," she said in a 2022 interview for Red Bull. "It bothered me that people thought I had no weaknesses. I then always believed that I must actually have no weaknesses. It put me under pressure." No one knew better than Ryf that all athletes—including her—have weaknesses, and she was bullshitting herself in attempting to believe what others believed about her. Going public with her fears was Ryf's way of taking them on, a wise move that took pressure off her so she could both feel better and perform better. And it worked. The following year, she set a new world record for the Ironman distance.

Honesty as Demandingness

Athletes like Daniela Ryf, who are honest with themselves even when it's most difficult, tend to prefer coaches who keep them honest—coaches they can count on to call out the self-deceptions they don't yet recognize. Take Karsten Warholm. In a 2019 interview for *Spikes*, the 400-meter hurdles world record holder spoke approvingly of the "tough love" approach of his coach, Leif Olav Alnes, recounting an episode where Alnes called him out for half-assing a workout Warholm thought he was crushing. "I really appreciate the honesty," Warholm said, "because I know it's coming from love. It's not him trying to push me down, it's him trying to lift me higher. Of course, he wouldn't say that to me if he knew that I was trying to do my best, but he knows that there is more potential. When I am not fulfilling my potential, he can be very harsh about that."

Being brutally honest with athletes as a coach is a manifestation of what sports psychologists like Andrea Becker of California State University, Fullerton call *demandingness*, or holding athletes to a high standard. In 2009, Becker conducted in-depth interviews with 18 athletes about their experiences with coaches, good and bad. The same 12 character traits kept coming up when these athletes talked about their favorite coaches, and chief among them were honesty and demandingness. When coaches hold athletes to a high standard, either by "keeping it real" or in other ways, it's because they believe in them, and athletes understand this. They feel seen, valued, challenged, and supported by such coaches.

It should be noted that Karsten Warholm and Leif Olav Alnes have a special relationship, which Warholm describes as "brotherly" despite the nearly 30-year age difference between them. Being "very harsh" works for these two, but in the majority of coach-athlete relationships, coaches need to find tactful means of being honest and direct when dropping truth bombs on athletes. Calling BS on a self-deceiving athlete achieves nothing if it's done in a clumsy way that causes them to feel attacked and judged and thus fails to effect the desired shift in perspective.

I once coached a runner named Abby, who kept finding reasons to delay or modify workouts. Though motivated and disciplined, she was seldom able to get her training done as planned. Individually, all of her excuses—fatigue, soreness, hectic workdays, poor sleep—were plausible, but collectively they defied the odds. Over time I began to suspect that Abby had an aversion to hard work, but this suspicion didn't hold water because the modified workouts she did weren't always easier than the ones I planned—they were just different.

One day it hit me that, for Abby, it was about control. Finding reasons to change the plan made her feel more in control of her workouts, and for whatever reason, this was important to her. In our next weekly check-in, I shared my insight with Abby, being careful not to dismiss any of her issues as invalid or fabricated while making it clear that I viewed them as secondary to the main issue of control. In these types of interactions, it's important for the coach to not only be sensitive and tactful but also to remember that they are not always right about everything, hence they need to approach athletes' apparent self-deceptions with intentional questions and "food for thought" types of statements instead of firm pronouncements. In this case, Abby readily owned that my hunch was on target, explaining that her need for control in training stemmed from a traumatic experience she'd had with an autocratic and punitive coach in high school. I thanked Abby for her openness and suggested we try a different angle on future planning that would account for her need for control. Rather than tell her exactly what to do and when, I would build some flexibility into the structure and timing of her workouts and allow her to decide on the specifics within the parameters I established.

It worked. My job became a lot easier, frankly, as Abby took advantage of the freedom afforded her to make her own adjustments. She seemed less anxious before big workouts and reported fewer mishaps. But most important, from my perspective, she became more honest with herself—and with me. Abby's "control thing" was now an acknowledged reality between us, something we worked with and through together in the same practical manner we would use to address any other limiter. I believe this marked a big step forward in her journey toward mastery.

Although self-deception might very well have evolved as an aid to deceiving others, it often serves an internal purpose, which is to protect us from seeing parts of ourselves we'd rather not see. The irony is that acknowledging the realities hidden behind our self-deceptions is often liberating, as we saw with Daniela Ryf. It allows us to relax the defense mechanisms we use to maintain our illusions and opens the door to real solutions. The truths we hide from ourselves are generally things that, if we saw them in someone else, we wouldn't judge negatively. In a sense, then, the job of the athlete who seeks to "keep it real" with themselves is to see themselves objectively. That's essentially what happened with Abby's need for control, a simple shift in perspective allowing her to say it just like that—"Abby has a need for control"—whereas previously it was more like, "I get anxious sometimes, and then a random finger cramp makes me decide it's necessary to change or delay a workout."

I don't want to take too much credit, but I can't help but wonder how long it would have taken Abby to effect this shift on her own, without the help of a coach. After all, the very nature of self-deception makes it difficult to self-correct. That's where journaling comes in. There's something about journaling that coaxes us to divulge our secrets, expressing thoughts we dare not think, much less express to others. Here's an example from the journal of Chrissie Wellington, who in a professional triathlon career spanning just five years won all thirteen of the iron-distance races she competed in: "I need to address some flaws in my personality. One of them is my tendency always to try to gain the approval and appreciation of others. I guess it's a reflection of my lack of self-confidence—needing constant reassurance."

Wellington makes it look easy, and in truth, keeping it real *is* easy. But first it's hard, and it remains hard until you learn to let go. It's kind of like skydiving, where falling—the thing you're afraid of—is the easy part, and choosing to leap is the hard part. I can't make that choice for you. I can only assure you that it's better to know the truth about yourself, and that the better you get at accepting and embracing reality overall—good and bad—the sooner you will arrive at endurance mastery.

FROM PRINCIPLE TO PRACTICE

You must overcome a natural tendency toward self-deception to conquer the challenges that threaten to impede your progress. Here are three ideas for turning this principle into practice on the path to mastery:

1/ Think of a time when you deceived yourself about something athletically and paid a cost. It might be the time you went faster than planned in a race because you "felt really good" and predictably hit the wall because absolutely nothing you did in your training suggested you were capable of sustaining that speed for the full distance. Or the time you stayed with a bad coach longer than you should have because you convinced yourself they were a good coach when really you couldn't muster the courage to fire the person. Or the time you burned yourself out training with a fitter partner because you wanted to believe you were just as fit. Whatever it is, take responsibility for both the self-deception and the fallout. This will make it easier for you to do the same in the future.

2/ Ask a coach or training partner or confidante who understands your sport if they see any ways you're limiting yourself as an athlete without realizing it. In other words, ask the person to call bullshit on you. If they can't think of anything right away, tell them to let you know when they do think of something, and when that happens, try not to be defensive. Sit with the idea and see what comes of it.

3/ Whenever something goes wrong for you athletically and it's not your fault, consider the possibility that you do bear some responsibility. Channel that inner skeptic who never lets any blunder pass unobserved, assuming you messed up until you've examined the evidence. The idea here is not to be mean to yourself but to act in your own best interest, knowing that we all deceive ourselves sometimes.

LESSON 22

Unsexy Restraint

I used to coach a runner who had a strong desire to impress me. After a solid workout performance, he would ask, "Hey Coach, were you impressed?" Or after botching a workout by pushing too hard in the beginning, he might say, "Sorry, Coach, I just wanted to impress you."

I felt two ways about these interactions. On the one hand, I recognized the runner's desire to impress me as a sign of respect. Generally speaking, we try to impress those whose good opinion we covet. On the other hand, it troubled me that the runner assumed I or any coach would be impressed with fast workout times. To me it betrayed a rather poor understanding of what coaches—good coaches, anyway—want to see from their athletes. So in the end I spoke up, explaining to the runner that, short of breaking a world record, there was nothing he could possibly do performance-wise in a workout that would impress me and he should stop trying.

In hindsight, I regret saying the part about world records, because even that wouldn't have impressed me in the way this runner hoped. Putting up strong numbers in workouts is evidence of talent more than anything else, and talent is not earned, it's a gift. To the extent that I am capable of being impressed by fast running, I am impressed by the giver of the gift (God, nature, whatever), not its recipient.

I don't mean to suggest that athletes should lack any desire to impress their coaches, or that coaches should never be impressed by anything an athlete does. After all, the desire to please one's coach is a powerful motivator for some athletes, and as we saw in Part I, maintaining a high level of motivation is critical to success in endurance sports. But crushing workouts is not the proper way for athletes to impress their coaches because again, it depends on something that is largely outside the athlete's control, which is innate ability.

In observing myself as a coach, I've noticed that when one of my athletes does impress me, it's always for one of two reasons, neither of which has anything to do with performance. The first is *grit*. An endurance athlete can't get very far without grit, and not all athletes have the amount required to master their sport. Consequently, when I see evidence of grit in an athlete I coach, I get happy.

One time an athlete of mine ran a 1-mile time trial in the middle of a city street because the sidewalks were blanketed in snow. A line of cars stacked up behind him during the six minutes it took him to complete the time trial, but he paid them no mind. My lawyers have advised me not to encourage this sort of behavior, but I can't help myself. I love that this athlete considered his running important enough to get a workout done in such an audacious manner. Anytime an athlete displays this level of grit, I reward them with what I call *commitment points*. While they lack exchange value, they serve the important purpose of letting athletes know their coach is impressed.

Grit is among the "sexier" virtues in endurance sports, I dare say. *Everyone* is impressed by grit. Angela Duckworth's book on grit was a national bestseller, and her TED Talk on the same subject has been viewed more than a million times. If you ask me, though, grit is a bit overhyped, which is why I'm even happier when an athlete demonstrates the second of the two traits that impress me as a coach, which is *restraint*.

Just Because You Can Doesn't Mean You Should

Restraint can mean a lot of things, but what I'm talking about is *self-restraint*, which psychologist Stephen Schroeder defined as "the ability to control one's impulses, emotions, or desires." This type of restraint is extremely useful in endurance sports—indeed, far more useful than most athletes recognize.

Why? It starts with motivation. We know that endurance athletes must be supremely motivated to reach their full potential—motivated enough to literally crawl across the finish line if need be. There is simply no such thing as being too motivated as an endurance athlete. Yet motivation alone does not enable athletes to get the most out of themselves. Crawling across the finish line shows poor judgment as much as it demonstrates motivation. An athlete who ends up in this position ought to have known better than to push as hard as they did, but lacking judgment, they allowed their motivation to run rampant and made dubious pacing decisions that landed them literally on their hands and knees.

Here's the thing, though: Even when athletes know better than to allow their motivation to go unchecked, they don't always check it. There's a difference between having good judgment and making good decisions. To have any effect on a situation, an athlete's good judgment must be *enacted*, and enacting good judgment isn't automatic. Think of all the scenarios in which a person has a clear understanding of what they should do and fails to do it. The taxpayer who knows they should start preparing their federal return in January but waits until April. The prediabetic who knows they should start exercising but keeps finding excuses not to. The workaholic who really means to spend more time with their family but continues to prioritize their career. It happens in sports as well. Most of the athletes I know who overtrain or blow up in races are fully aware that they are sabotaging themselves by failing to act on their better judgment.

Restraint is the psychological midwife that enables an athlete to act on their better judgment, checking their motivation when it needs to be checked. It might not be the sexiest athletic virtue (in fact, it's definitely not), but restraint is every bit as important as motivation and judgment in the quest to achieve sport mastery, and that's why it never fails to impress me when it's exercised by an athlete I'm coaching.

The preferred scientific term for restraint is *self-control*. You also see it referred to sometimes as *inhibitory control*. Whatever you call it, research indicates that restraint predicts success in sports, with champion athletes exhibiting greater self-control than lesser athletes. A 2020 study published in the *Journal of Sport and Exercise Physiology* found that inhibitory control (as measured by the widely used Stop Signal Task) was strongly associated with competitive performance in a group of more than 100 athletes representing a variety of sports. Simply put, athletes who are good at holding themselves back generally tend to also be good at whatever sport they compete in.

Self-control comes in two flavors: the aforementioned inhibitory form and its inverse, *initiatory control*. Both entail overriding impulses in pursuit of goals, but they work in opposite directions. As the name suggests, initiatory control enables a person to override internal resistance to commencing or continuing a behavior, whereas inhibitory control helps a person override the impulse to keep doing something when their goal is to stop. A person who wants to lose weight, for example, requires initiatory control to start and maintain a walking habit and inhibitory control to reduce their fast-food consumption.

Initiatory control is the more familiar flavor of self-control, justly appreciated by athletes and coaches alike. A study of 398 teenagers and young adults training for a marathon found that those who started out with higher levels of initiatory control (which in this case manifested as the ability to get out the door and run when they really didn't want to) tended to perform better on race day, and that those whose initiatory control declined in the course of training performed worse.

It's important to note that the runners in this study were mostly first-time marathoners involved in a fundraising effort. Hence, they likely weren't as intrinsically motivated as the typical competitive runner. Initiatory control is most valuable when motivation is low, supplying the *oomph* to do something you'd rather not do. But when motivation is high, there's not much need for initiatory control because there's little or no internal resistance to overcome. A 2020 study led by Ian Taylor of Loughborough University found that, within a group of 40 athletes, those who scored higher on a measure of autonomous motivation reported "lower temptation to reduce effort and higher value of goal pursuit" in a 10-minute cycling task and also performed better. These athletes felt less tempted to quit because they were more motivated, and because they felt less tempted to quit, they didn't need to exercise much initiatory control to keep pushing.

By the same token, higher levels of motivation demand more inhibitory control (i.e., restraint) from athletes. A 2015 study by Italian researchers measured inhibitory control in a group of ultrarunners. Those who recorded higher scores in a test of inhibitory control performed better in a trail race than their less restrained counterparts. Although pacing was not analyzed in this study, it's likely that superior pacing partially mediated the relationship between inhibitory control and performance, as it is well established that higher finishers in ultramarathons slow down significantly less as the race unfolds than do lower finishers. In other words, they do a better job of holding themselves back.

I've spent a lot of time around elite endurance athletes in my career, and I can tell you that, by and large, they are masters of restraint. In fact, it's been my observation that the most striking psychological difference between elite and non-elite endurance athletes is that the former are much better at holding themselves back when appropriate. Whereas non-elite athletes tend to try to *beat* their target times in interval workouts, elites try to *nail* their times. And while non-elite athletes are prone to gutting their way through disastrous workouts, elites are quick to abandon them in the spirit of living to fight another day. The same goes for dealing with niggles, those painful warnings of potential injury, which non-elite athletes often ignore and try to push through, in contrast to the elites, who almost always heed these warnings with responsive adjustments to their training.

Similar caution is shown by elite athletes at broader timescales, where escalating fatigue is interpreted as a sign of working too hard and not—as many non-elites see it—a sign of working hard enough. An example is middle-distance runner Jakob Ingebrigtsen of Norway, who by the age of 24 had won six Olympic and World Championship medals at 1500 and 5000 meters, four of them gold. In training, Ingebrigtsen relies heavily on blood lactate testing to regulate the intensity of his workouts, which are often done on a treadmill for further control. But while fans fixate on the lactate tests, they're not really the point. "The real differentiator and guiding principle," wrote former elite miler Kyle Merber in an analysis of Ingebrigtsen's approach, "is that no individual session should ever be so hard as to risk injury or compromise the next. It's a tempered and long-term-oriented approach that relies on stacking general fitness versus bombing a Hail Mary at the end of the season."

My message for you is this: To reach your full potential, you must take a cue from Jakob Ingebrigtsen and embrace restraint, despite its unsexiness. Make it your "thing"—a special advantage you hold over athletes who focus on grit and other sexy virtues at the expense of judgment and restraint. Model your training after that of the great

Eliud Kipchoge, the two-time Olympic Marathon champion, who said in a 2021 interview for *Outside*, "I try not to run 100 percent. I perform 80 percent on Tuesday, Thursday, and Saturday and then at 50 percent Monday, Wednesday, Friday, and Sunday." When a lesser runner passes you on the bike path, take pride in resisting the temptation to show them who's boss. Ignore the self-sabotaging pseudo-competition of Strava. Give yourself a pat on the back when you bail out of a workout that isn't going well and are rewarded with a strong and healthy performance in your next workout. Smile inwardly when you see other runners fail to exercise restraint, and feed your special advantage. Tattoo your brain with the motto, "Just because you can doesn't mean you should."

FROM PRINCIPLE TO PRACTICE

Restraint is a signature trait of endurance mastery, enabling athletes to make decisions that are consistent with their best judgment. Here are three ideas for turning this principle into practice on the path to mastery:

1/ Sit down with your journal and write about a time when you failed to exercise restraint, acted against your better judgment, and suffered the consequences. Perhaps you tried to rebound too quickly from a disappointing marathon knowing it was risky and wound up injured. (I did!) Now imagine you get a do-over and describe what you would do differently and why.

2/ Now shift your perspective from the past to the future and identify the type of situation in which you most often fail to exercise restraint as an athlete. Is it not slowing down when you know you're pushing too hard in a low-intensity training session? Not resting when your body is clearly telling you it needs rest? Snacking on energy bars instead of having a proper lunch? Whatever it is, devise a plan for holding yourself back the next time you encounter the same temptation.

3/ Make a note of each time you hold yourself back when you should and each time you fail to act upon your best judgment. Give yourself a point when you exercise restraint and subtract a point when you don't. See how many points you can accrue in a week.

Personal Best

Joseph Conrad's novella *The Secret Sharer* tells the story of a young sea captain who finds himself in the awkward position of assuming command of a British sailing vessel he's never set foot on that is crewed by a tight-knit group of seamen who've been together for years. Though confident in his abilities, the rookie skipper hopes to prove himself "faithful to that ideal conception of one's own personality that every man sets up for himself secretly." The story goes on to show the young captain striving to do precisely this in the face of even greater challenges than the one that concerns him in this moment of reflection.

The relevance of Conrad's novella to your athletic interests is that, although the stakes are lower, sports challenge people to be faithful to their ideal self-image in much the same way the young sea captain's difficulties challenged him to be faithful to his. The greatest athletes often describe the quest to become the best athlete they can be as inseparable from the quest to become the best person they can be. An example is Timothy Bradley Jr., who celebrated his 2022 induction into the International Boxing Hall of Fame by penning an open letter to his younger self that speaks to the link between personal and athletic development. "Over the next few years," Bradley wrote, "you are going to make mistakes. Don't worry. We all make mistakes. Please don't get upset, Tim. No one is perfect. You are young and still trying to find yourself. But if you can admit your faults, you should be willing to change. Perhaps you will become more assertive, focused, and aware in making sound decisions, heightening mindfulness to make better choices expeditiously, confidently, and without hesitation."

It is clear from examples like this one that personal growth and athletic development really do go hand in hand. And I believe this is especially true in endurance sports. Six-time Ironman world champion Mark Allen once described endurance racing as "a test of you as a person on top of a test of you as an athlete." If he's right about this (and who are we to doubt him?), then to become the best athlete one can be, one must also become the best version of oneself.

Perhaps you're skeptical about this. After all, the relationship between personal and athletic development is not immediately obvious. But it starts to make sense when we study the work of Carl Rogers and other psychologists interested in human potential. In the 1950s, Rogers coined the term *self-concept* to refer to the way we see ourselves as individuals. The main components of this global view of the self are self-image (how we perceive our bodies), self-esteem (how highly we regard ourselves), social comparisons (how we stack up against others), and ideal self, or who we strive to become. Rogers believed that humans possess a natural drive toward congruence, where the various components of self-concept bind together into a cohesive whole and merge with the ideal self.

Closely related to Rogers's notion of congruence is Abraham Maslow's concept of self-actualization. The key difference is that, whereas Rogers saw personal growth as mostly a matter of maturing in character, Maslow (whom you may recall as the inspiration for Stephen Seiler's hierarchy of endurance training needs in Lesson 11) viewed it as mainly a matter of developing skills and abilities. Self-actualization "may be loosely described as the full use and exploitation of talents, capabilities, potentialities, etc." Maslow wrote. "Such people seem to be fulfilling themselves and to be doing the best that they are capable of doing. They are people who have developed or are developing to the full stature of which they are capable."

Recent research by psychologist Scott Barry Kaufman suggests that self-actualization encompasses both character and abilities. Through rigorous testing of the 17 traits that Maslow associated with self-actualization, Kaufman identified 10 that stand up to scientific scrutiny. A number of these 10 traits have to do with personal character. They include authenticity ("I can maintain my dignity and integrity even in environments and situations that are undignified"), purpose ("I feel a great responsibility and duty to accomplish a particular mission in life"), humanitarianism ("I have a genuine desire to help the human race"), and moral intuition ("I can tell 'deep down' right away when I've done something wrong").

Interestingly, Kaufman's research also revealed that people who exhibit a high level of character through traits like moral intuition also tend to perform better at work and have higher levels of skill development, validating the beliefs of Timothy Bradley Jr. and other great athletes. And it's not just great athletes who understand the link between character and performance. Coaches do too. "For me, success is not about the wins and losses," said English Premier League soccer coach Ted Lasso. "It's about helping these young fellas be the best versions of themselves on and off the field."

Granted, Ted Lasso is a fictional character who doesn't exist except on television. But a number of notable real-life coaches have said essentially the same thing. Three-time Super Bowl-winning football coach Bill Walsh tellingly titled his book on leadership *The Score Takes Care of Itself*. When Walsh took the helm of the San Francisco

49ers in 1979 following a dismal two-win season, he instituted a code he called the Standards of Performance. Among its 17 tenets were "Demonstrate respect for each person in the organization," "Show self-control, especially under pressure," and "Demonstrate character."

Walsh held every player to the same high standard, regardless of tenure or stature. Egotism drove him up the wall, as a star offensive lineman learned in what would be his last season with the team. Having defied tenet number 15 ("Put the team's welfare and priorities ahead of my own") once too often, the player's ill-timed demand for a pay raise was answered with a cardboard box in which he was instructed to place all of his locker-room belongings.

Character Drives Winning

Most of us would agree that, in the bigger picture, character is more important than winning. But what coaches like Bill Walsh understand is that character drives winning. The surest way to score more points than your opponent is to focus on building a winning character and let the score take care of itself. The caveat is that character drives winning only for those *who also care a lot about winning* (and by "winning" I really mean "performance," as not every athlete is capable of winning in the literal sense). That's the beauty of sport: When an athlete commits to reaching their full potential, they embrace a journey in which they are guaranteed to fail on occasion, and some of these failures will be self-inflicted, blamable on flaws or weaknesses in the athlete's character. In this way, sport confronts athletes with images of who they *don't* want to be, and from there's it's just one small step to gaining insight into who they *do* want to be.

I've shared how fear drove me to failure in my high school running career, a painful experience that had the compensatory benefit of teaching me that fearlessness was integral to my ideal self. When I returned to running as an adult, chasing personal-best race performances became my chosen instrument for chasing my personal-best self, something all true seekers of mastery do in one way or another.

Failure is not the only catalyst for this process. Unhappiness also does the trick. In 2019, professional runner Grayson Murphy signed a contract with Northern Arizona Elite, the pro team I'd been fortunate to train two years earlier, which was the opportunity of a lifetime for the 23-year-old recent college graduate—or so she thought. Yet despite performing well, Murphy chafed against the hyperfocused lifestyle she felt compelled to conform to as a member of the team. A spike in anxiety, which she'd been prone to throughout her life, was the final clue that she needed to make a change. "Ultimately," she wrote on her blog, "I came to the conclusion that while running plays a major role in my life, it will never be my whole life. For better or worse, I am a person who needs more than running in my life to be fulfilled and feel happy." So Murphy moved home to Utah to become the person she felt she needed to be, taking up a more balanced lifestyle that included entrepreneurship, socializing, mental health advocacy, and other sports, such as mountain climbing. The effect on her main sport of running was profoundly positive, leading Grayson to four national championship titles and two world championship gold medals in mountain running.

Psychologists refer to the process Grayson Murphy underwent as *transformational learning*. It occurs when a person experiences a "disorienting event" that challenges certain core beliefs. Endurance races often function as disorienting events, as Timothy Gillum of the University of Missouri–St. Louis discovered in researching a 2009 doctoral study that looked for evidence of transformational learning in recreational runners training for and completing a marathon. Among them was "Meb" (a pseudonym), who, despite a poor performance, came away from the race feeling "stronger and better" than he had in some time. "I went into this just wanting to get my confidence back, and I had one of the worst races of my life," he told Gillum. "And I feel better about running [now] than I ever have before. I don't know. It sort of regrouped me somehow. I found my center again. I didn't really stop. I took four days off and went right back into it." These are the words of an athlete who intends to be more like the person who finished the race than the person who started it.

The reflective element of transformational learning is critical. Experiencing a disorienting event such as an intense race does not alone guarantee transformation. You must also use the event as an opportunity to gain insight into yourself. This is more likely to happen if you're already in the habit of reflecting on where you are in your growth journey and where you want to go. In a biography of Kenyan running coach Patrick Sang, author Sarah Gearhart writes, "In his mind, an athlete is not just an athlete. 'Who are you?' is the root question he wants each person he coaches to consider." This is not a question that any of us can answer once and then move on to other questions, like a contestant on some trivia game show. Human identity is far too complex and changeable for that.

According to modern neuroscience, there is in fact no such thing as a single, unified self. Each of us contains many selves, and in pursuing mastery, athletes catch glimpses of a congruent preferred self, which over time becomes an ever-evolving standard they aspire to and gradually approach without ever fully attaining. Like Patrick Sang, I continuously encourage the athletes I coach to meditate on these matters as they navigate the many challenges their sport throws at them. In doing so, they not only handle these challenges more skillfully but also benefit more from the overall experience, making faster progress toward becoming the best versions of themselves.

There's an exercise called the Best Possible Self intervention that you can use to formalize this process. Developed by psychologist Laura King in 2001, BPS is a reflective writing exercise that prompts participants to be specific about who they want to be and what their life would be like if they became this person. According to a scientific review published in 2019, there is strong evidence that BPS has positive short-term effects on well-being, optimism, and mood.

That's nice, but what athletes are looking for is a long-term positive effect on personal character and sport mastery. To this end, I recommend that you periodically revisit the exercise, perhaps at the conclusion of each competitive season. The young captain in Conrad's novella kept the "ideal conception of his own personality" a secret, and (spoiler alert) it worked out okay. But it's preferable for athletes and coaches to express openly who they want to be. Putting it out there creates an accountability that gives all seekers of endurance mastery the greatest chance of achieving their personal best as athletes and as human beings.

FROM PRINCIPLE TO PRACTICE

In order to become the best athlete you can be, you must work toward becoming the best person you can be. Here are three ideas for turning this principle into practice on the path to mastery:

1/ Take a few minutes to imagine a future you who's successfully become the person you want to be. What is that person like? How do they act, feel, and think? In what specific ways are they different from your current self? How does this person affect others? And most importantly for our purposes, what is this person able to achieve as an athlete or coach by virtue of being the best possible version of you? Answer these questions in writing, being as concrete, detailed, and realistic as possible. Finish the exercise by explaining how you will become the best version of yourself.

2/ Before each race, ask yourself what it means for you to compete as the best version of yourself. Make it your primary goal to prove faithful to this ideal conception of yourself, ahead of all performance goals.

3/ Every few months, evaluate your progress toward becoming your best possible self, identify the area where you need the most work, and come up with one or more specific steps you can take to further your progress.

What's Your Pebble?

A few years ago, America's second-largest pharmacy chain launched an advertising campaign with the tagline, "Walgreens is all about making life easier." If the words sound familiar, it's because versions of the same catchphrase have been used by dozens of other brands over the years, which tells me that the average consumer finds the prospect of an easier life appealing. The science of commercial advertising is just that—a science—and major corporations don't reuse old messaging without proof of its effectiveness.

I suppose any rational consumer wants the process of getting their prescriptions filled to be as easy as possible. But assuming Walgreens delivers on this promise, are they actually making our lives easier? And to the extent that our lives have been made easier by products and services that address our daily hassles, are we happier than we were when life was harder?

Science says otherwise. Studies of historical trends in psychological well-being suggest that the average person has become neither more nor less satisfied with life over the generations. Your great-grandparents missed out on drone grocery delivery, but odds are you're no happier than they were. And if you're not, then Walgreens is lying to us. Products and services don't make our lives easier in any meaningful way, nor does easy living make us happier.

Sigmund Freud knew this a century ago. In his 1929 book *Civilization and Its Discontents*, Freud argues that the recalcitrant nature of human happiness makes it impossible for us to technologize our way out of our natural state of existential angst. "If there had been no railway to conquer distances," he writes in a famous passage, "my child would never have left his native town and I should need no telephone to hear his voice." In short, every solution creates a new problem, leaving us right where we started happiness-wise.

The Buddha knew the same thing in the second century B.C.E. According to legend, Siddhartha Gautama (aka the Buddha) was raised by wealthy and overprotective parents who tried to make their son's life as easy as possible. But an easy life did not bring lasting happiness to the young prince, and when confronted with the inescapable realities of sickness, aging, and death, he renounced the easy life and went searching for happiness, a journey of purposeful self-challenge that became the very source of his happiness.

People want life to be easy. That's why advertisers promise to make our lives easier, and why the Buddha's parents raised him inside a protective bubble. But people also want to be happy, and it turns out that easy living doesn't yield happiness, whereas purposeful self-challenge does. Psychologists call this the *effort paradox*. In a 2018 paper on the subject, Michael Inzlicht of the University of Colorado observed that, although humans have a well-documented tendency to minimize effort in a variety of situations, "Effort can [also] be experienced as valuable or rewarding in its own right. While humans and other animals readily apply more effort for better outcomes, they sometimes view the same outcomes as more rewarding if more (not less) effort was used to attain them." As an example, Inzlicht notes that "mountaineers value mountain climbing precisely because it is so arduous and effortful."

It's no accident that the most effortful sports of all—endurance sports—went mainstream in the 1970s, the decade of microwave meals and waterbeds. According to sociologist Michael Atkinson, life became too damn easy for many people around this time, and they went berserk. Suffocating beneath the coddling softness of an American dream turned nightmare, vast numbers of modern-day Buddhas extricated themselves from their La-Z-Boys and came together in so-called pain communities, chasing a feeling Atkinson termed "exciting significance."

"People are really tired of living a sort of dull, boring, and sedentary lifestyle," he told me in a 2010 interview. "Most triathletes have white-collar desk jobs. They don't use their bodies. They use their minds or their voices all day, and they really like the physical aspect of doing something grueling like triathlon." A triathlete himself, Atkinson interviewed members of his own pain community—a local triathlon club—for a paper titled "Triathlon, Suffering, and Exciting Significance." Among them was Oliver, a middle manager and family man who did nothing more strenuous in his daily life than operate a television remote control until he took up triathlon, which cured him of a soul-sapping ennui. "I had money," he explained to Atkinson. "I had stability; but I had nothing to make me feel alive, to make my body and mind work in different ways. I think that's the essence of being human, to feel alive, to move beyond the comforts of familiarity. It's about saying to yourself that you don't want to feel dead on earth."

Degrees of Challenge

Oliver's right, of course. As humans we possess an innate drive to challenge ourselves. That's why so many of us choose to become endurance athletes. But even the endorphin junkies among us also tend to avoid discomfort and minimize unnecessary effort, which is why we invent and use things like La-Z-Boys and remote controls. And when they are combined in an athlete, these opposing instincts—challenge-seeking and laziness—yield individuals who really want to test themselves . . . but only to a point.

I took a poll on social media, asking my fellow athletes how often they finish a race feeling they gave everything they had and could not have gone any faster by digging any deeper. Only 7.7 percent of respondents answered "always," while another 70 percent admitted they seldom or never go all out in races. "I probably have the capacity to push more," commented one athlete, "and no reason not to, and yet I just don't, or I seem to forget."

Another example of this lukewarm embrace of challenge is the rising appeal of "easy" marathons like the downhill REVEL Race Series. There's nothing wrong with seeking beginner-friendly courses where fast times are guaranteed, but it's worth questioning yourself if the reason you got into endurance sports was that you craved a challenge, and now here you are trying to minimize the challenge for the sake of putting up numbers that enhance your status.

And it's not just amateurs who bring this lukewarm attitude to their respective pain communities. When USA Track & Field announced a noon start time for the 2024 Olympic Trials Marathon in Orlando, Florida, a vocal faction of qualifiers protested, arguing that the expected afternoon high temperature of 73°F (cooler than almost any of the marathons that Ironman triathletes endure on summer afternoons after having already swum 2.4 miles and cycled 112 miles) was too warm. These elite athletes were okay with the challenge of running 26.2 miles, but any challenge beyond that was totally unacceptable.

Chosen and Unchosen Challenges

Let's be clear: Some challenges are chosen, others unchosen. Becoming an endurance athlete is a choice, but many of the challenges athletes face in pursuit of improvement are unchosen. In my experience, most endurance athletes have little tolerance for unchosen challenges. When they get injured or go through a rough patch in training or struggle with their nutrition, they react like entitled consumers storming back to Walmart with their defective robot vacuums, demanding refunds. They love the challenge of chasing improvement as endurance athletes . . . as long as everything goes their way.

I said most athletes, mind you, not all. When Courtney Dauwalter lost her vision in the middle of the 2017 Run Rabbit Run 100-mile trail race, she kept running—and won. At no point did she even consider stopping, instead treating her sudden (and thankfully temporary) blindness as just another part of the overall challenge of running 100 miles. Eliud Kipchoge had a similar reaction when his left shoe spontaneously fell apart during the 2015 Berlin Marathon, shrugging off the mishap after winning the race despite a bloodied foot. "That is sport," he told reporters. "I had pain in my foot, but what could I do? I had to finish the race." And when social media exploded with grumbling about the Olympic Trials Marathon noon start time, two-time Olympian Des Linden openly mocked the grumblers, which she rightly characterized as a freely bestowed competitive advantage to tougher competitors like herself. It's probably no coincidence that Linden won the 2018 Boston Marathon in famously hellacious weather conditions that caused quite a bit of whining from others in the race.

Again, there's nothing wrong with choosing a flat course and hoping the weather cooperates when you're going after a personal-best race time. Nor is there anything wrong with racing for finisher's medals rather than for personal bests, doing just enough to break free from La-Z-Boy inertia and experience exciting significance. The problem comes when athletes who claim to want to reach their full potential set a limit on their challenge-seeking, as only those who consistently challenge themselves to the absolute maximum have any hope of achieving mastery.

Challenges are to athletic development as soil, water, and sunlight are to plants. You grow as an athlete to the exact degree you challenge yourself, and fall short of your potential to the exact degree you avoid challenges. If you challenge yourself 90 percent as much as you could, you are fulfilling 90 percent of your potential. It's as simple as that.

The thing that trips up a lot of athletes is that challenges have a different relationship to performance than they have to mastery. Challenges are the enemy of performance in the sense that, when the weather's terrible, race times suffer. But they are the friend of mastery, because self-regulatory ability grows in direct response to embracing challenges. In chasing performance instead of mastery (for example, by running only marathons with net-downhill courses), athletes avoid challenges, thereby slowing their progress toward mastery and ultimately limiting their performance.

Such athletes would do well to study certain other sports, particularly bouldering, where the inseparability of challenge, performance, and mastery is impossible to overlook. Ask a boulderer how good they are and they will answer with a number on the V scale, which ranks individual climbs (or "problems" as they're aptly known within the sport) by degree of difficulty. Improvement in bouldering entails moving up the V scale by continuously attacking problems one level above one's current level. There is only one road to better performance, and that's the road of bigger challenges. In endurance sports, however, athletes can pursue performance at the expense of growth by taking the easy way, but as in bouldering, only the hard way leads to true mastery.

I'm not saying you have to make things as hard as possible all the time. Training in combat boots is harder than training in running shoes, but it's also dumb. Here's the thing, though: To run the very best race you're capable of, you have to make the race as hard as you can by trying as hard as you can. Even if you've chosen the fastest course available, the weather is perfect, you're wearing carbon-plated super shoes, a hired pacer is pacing you, and you're hopped up on performance-enhancing supplements, you cannot reach the finish line in the least time possible without challenging yourself to actually do this, and the few who do are the few who exhibit a challenge-seeking mindset not only on race day but every day.

I'll leave you with one more example of such an athlete: Kara Goucher, another two-time Olympian, who throughout her career refused to stop and remove pebbles from her shoes during training runs. Even if she noticed a pebble or other debris when she put the shoe on, before she'd even started her run, she'd leave it be, regarding the small nuisance as good practice for races, where stopping for any reason could cost her victory.

The pebble is not the point. Goucher's husband and fellow Olympian, Adam, thought she was crazy for leaving pebbles in her shoes, but he found other ways to challenge himself. What's your pebble?

FROM PRINCIPLE TO PRACTICE

Despite their challenge-seeking nature, endurance athletes also have a natural human tendency to avoid hard efforts, which prevents many from reaching their full potential, and only those who challenge themselves to the absolute maximum achieve mastery. Here are three ideas for turning this principle into practice on the path to mastery:

1/ Pull out your journal and write about your relationship with self-challenge. Did you become an endurance athlete because you liked the challenge? Has this changed over time? Do you always give everything you've got in races, and if you don't, do you wish you did? Do you sometimes take the easy way out or complain about the unchosen challenges you encounter as an athlete? Don't judge yourself in answering these and similar questions. The goal is to gain clarity on where you are and where you want to go in your challenge-seeking.

2/ Think of a way in which you could benefit from challenging yourself more. An example is switching from the familiar, rote strength workouts you do on your own to a coached strength class that's much harder and more effective. Now make it happen!

3/ Try to go an entire month without complaining about a single unchosen, sport-related challenge, such as bad weather, difficult training routes, muscle pain, disappointing numbers, and technology fails. See what effect this has on your overall attitude toward challenge and effort.

More with Less

eon Fleisher never ran a marathon or swam the English Channel or raced a bike. Nevertheless, his story offers a valuable lesson to endurance athletes. Born in 1928 to Jewish immigrants living in San Francisco, Fleisher started playing the piano at age 4, advancing so rapidly that within five years he'd caught the attention of renowned composer Artur Schnabel, who became his teacher. At 16, Fleisher made his Carnegie Hall debut, and by his mid-twenties he was widely considered to be among the greatest pianists of his generation.

Then tragedy struck. At 36, Fleisher mysteriously lost the use of his right hand. We all value our hands, but few depend on these appendages more than a celebrated concert pianist, and for Fleisher the strange and sudden paralysis of his five-fingered moneymaker was devastating. Yet despite his understandable anguish, he showed admirable resilience and adaptability in coping with the affliction. Fleisher tried just about everything to restore function to his hand— lidocaine, rehabilitation therapy, psychotherapy, shock treatments, Rolfing, EST—and when nothing worked, he shifted some of his energies into teaching and conducting. Meanwhile, he continued to play, mastering a repertoire of compositions written for the left hand and commissioning others, which he performed at sold-out concerts and in critically acclaimed recordings. In interviews, Fleisher often intimated that losing the use of his right hand expanded his creativity and forced him to think more deeply about music, telling one reporter, "Limitations are the food of the creator" (a line he attributed to the great German writer Johann von Goethe).

There's no evidence that Goethe actually penned this aphorism, but his equal in artistic stature, Leonardo da Vinci, made precisely the same point in his posthumously published notebooks, writing, "Art lives from constraints and dies from freedom." Counterintuitive though this notion may be to some, science supports it. In a 2022 paper titled "Creativity from Constraints: Theory and Application," Rider University psychologists Catrinel Tromp and John Baer observed that "studies on constraints in creativity show that . . . more creative outcomes often emerge under more constrained conditions that allow *less* choice." When artists are given a lot of freedom in their work, they naturally revert to familiar tendencies. But when intrusive or even arbitrary limitations are imposed on how they create, their minds are compelled to explore, and the resulting output is often more original.

A great example is Theodor Geisel, better known as Dr. Seuss. In 1960, Random House publisher Bennett Cerf challenged the children's author to write a successful follow-up to his bestselling debut, *The Cat in the Hat*, using no more than 50 different words. Seuss embraced the challenge, and with great success, making clever use of repetition to produce *Green Eggs and Ham*, a classic story-in-rhyme made up of precisely 50 different words.

Constraints facilitate creativity not just in the arts but also in sports. This was demonstrated in a 2014 study by Anita Haudum and colleagues at the University of Salzburg. The constraint in this particular experiment was quite literal, consisting of a rubber tube that runners attached to their hip and ankle and wore for seven weeks, during which time they completed 18 treadmill runs. Blood lactate and muscle activation levels were measured to determine how hard the runners' muscles were working at a fixed speed at three different time points: 1) before the constraint was introduced; 2) during their first run with the rubber tubing; and 3) after seven weeks of practice. As expected, blood lactate and muscle activation levels were elevated during the first run completed with the rubber tubing. Seven weeks later, though, these measurements were almost back down to baseline, indicating that the runners had learned to alter their biomechanics in a way that compensated for the constraint.

You might be wondering how this experiment is relevant to real-world endurance training. After all, athletes are not in the habit of randomly imposing external mechanical constraints on their bodies. True enough, but it's also true that the body is always changing, and as the body changes, the internal constraints that limit fitness and performance change also. In particular, aging causes athletes to become increasingly constrained by changes in their organs and tissues. The muscles lose contractile force, the tendons and ligaments become stiffer, heart rate variability and maximal heart rate decrease, the immune system dysregulates, and the brain becomes less plastic. Athletes who experience these and other aging-related changes find themselves struggling to get the usual results from the usual practices.

People who say that age is just a number are kidding themselves. Age is biology. But biology is complex, and it is only one piece of the performance puzzle. The science of constraints offers hope to us athletes who aren't as young as we used to be. From this perspective, aging is just another constraint-driven opportunity to adapt and get better. By pushing back creatively against the biological encroachments of age, you can do more with less, as the saying goes.

A case in point is Meb Keflezighi, who started running competitively at age 13 and ran his best race a full quarter of a century later. Meb's competitive résumé was already stacked with fine performances when he lined up for the start of the 2014 Boston Marathon just two weeks shy of his 39th birthday. He'd won a bronze medal in the 2004 Olympics, taken first place at the 2009 New York City Marathon, and crowned himself champion of the 2012 US Olympic Trials Marathon. But his winning time of 2:08:37 at Boston was a lifetime best, and it made him the oldest winner of that hallowed event since 1930. There's no question that Meb was past his physical prime when he achieved his greatest victory. But he knew this better than anyone, and he'd adapted in ways that enabled him to keep improving even after his body had begun to decline.

In his twenties, Meb ate a lot of fast food, and by all appearances he got away with it. Those empty calories simply vanished, vaporized by 120-mile training weeks. Fast-forward a decade, and this was no longer the case. Increasingly, the fat Meb ate become the fat he carried on his petite frame, so he overhauled his diet, replacing burgers and fries with fruits, nuts, wheat toast, egg whites, fish, and other unprocessed foods. Quite apart from the beneficial impact these changes had on Meb's body composition, his transition from an "anything goes" diet to textbook eating undoubtedly made him healthier in general, and as we've seen, health is the foundation of fitness.

On the training side, the biggest accommodation Meb made to his aging body was a shift from traditional seven-day microcycles to nine-day cycles, which afforded him more time to recover between workouts. Further adjustments were made in response to how Meb was feeling, something he hadn't done as much of when he was younger. "I can't do the workouts I did twelve years ago," he said in a 2016 interview for *Forbes*. "Now it's more in moderation. I listen to my body and know what it needs."

Two distinct strategies are represented in Meb's responses to aging. His diet overhaul was a way of removing slack from his habits by tightening things up a bit. Meb could have benefited from making the same changes earlier, but he was not motivated to do so until new constraints threatened his ability to perform at his accustomed level. Meb's training modifications, meanwhile, were a matter of bending to the realities of his aging body. Being inflexible in his performance standards required him to become more flexible in his training methods in the face of these realities.

It's a Mindset Thing

The purpose of this chapter is not to supply a bunch of tips on aging successfully as an endurance athlete. My goal, rather, is to explain the underlying mindset required to do more with less as an athlete. Getting older creates an opportunity for athletes like you only inasmuch as you seize this opportunity by refusing to slow down and opening yourself up to making whatever changes are required to avoid slowing down. Tips are relatively worthless on their own. An athlete who lacks Meb Keflezighi's mindset toward aging won't make very good use of the tips they receive, while an athlete who has this mindset is bound to figure out how to adapt, with or without the tips. This is true not only for aging but for all aspects of chasing mastery in endurance sports. Athletes don't reach their full potential by absorbing and applying information; they get there by learning how to self-regulate.

Of course, every athlete slows down sooner or later. But remember, performance and mastery are two different things. Performance comes partly from factors that are beyond the athlete's control, such as youth and genetic makeup. But mastery comes from making good decisions consistently. An athlete who is young and gifted may perform at a high level that is nevertheless nowhere near their full potential, whereas an athlete who is well past their physical prime and getting slower might still be moving closer to mastery.

I know whereof I speak. When I lined up for the Atlanta Marathon in 2020, I was 48 years old and no longer capable of producing a personal best time at this distance, especially on a course with more than 1,800 feet of elevation gain. But I *was* capable of controlling my thoughts, emotions, and actions in the service of my goals, and the result was that, of the 2,101 other runners in the race, only thirteen finished ahead of me, the oldest of whom was eight years my junior. More important, I finished knowing I couldn't possibly have done any better. If you ask me, there is no greater experience for an endurance athlete at any age than knowing you've gotten absolutely everything out of yourself. When you've mastered your sport, you can feel it, and it feels terrific.

FROM PRINCIPLE TO PRACTICE

Constraints—including the constraint of aging—present athletes with opportunities to improve, provided they are embraced as such. Here are three ideas for turning this principle into practice on the path to mastery:

1/ Ask yourself whether there are any constraints you operate under that you could turn from a limiter to an advantage by being resourceful. Suppose you have an unconventional work schedule that makes it impossible for you to follow a normal Monday-to-Sunday schedule. How might you balance work and rest in a way that makes the most of best opportunities to train? Other examples include making the most of equipment limitations, environmental constraints, traveling, or being stuck indoors in bad weather.

2/ Consider whether there is any slack in your current routine that you've more or less gotten away with up to this point but that you could benefit from tightening up now, before it becomes a more pressing constraint. Perhaps it's time to give more than lip service to mobility work, mental skills training, or performance nutrition.

3/ Regardless of how old you are or how long you've been competing, think about where you would like to be in five years. In what ways do you hope to be better as an athlete? Identify one thing you can change now to chart a more direct path to the future you envision.

EPILOGUE

The purpose of this book has been to offer a conceptual framework that helps athletes like you master their sport and reach their full potential. It's not easy. Athletic development in the fullest sense means cultivating the capacity to self-regulate in ways that turn every last drop of your potential into performance. This is far more difficult than simply doing a lot of good training and reaping the results, which is how athletic development is typically thought of.

Yet as difficult as mastering a sport may be, I would like to think you're in a better position now than you were when you started this book. The mere fact that you recognize mastery as the ultimate objective in endurance sports puts you well ahead of most athletes, for whom fulfillment of potential is at best an implicit goal and often not even that. Making this goal explicit changes how you think about and approach athletic development. The name of the game is making good decisions, and good decisions are made by those who are good at self-regulating.

Nobody becomes a champion self-regulator overnight. It's a process. And for endurance athletes specifically, there are five pillars of mastery that maximize athlete development and facilitate training and racing at full potential. Let's review:

The first pillar is **motivation**, wherein you recognize that the extent of your love for your sport is correlated with how far you will go in it; you know the limit of endurance performance is perceptual in nature rather than physical, and only the most motivated athletes ever find their perceptual limit; you target your motivational sweet spot by ensuring your current training is "hard fun"; you seek out environments that are conducive to endurance sport success and performance; and you embrace the notion of conquering fear as an endurance athlete.

The second pillar is **learning**, guided by the tenant of putting health before fitness; a realization that whatever your experience or ability, you can take cues from elite best practices; a commitment to working with coaches and other experts who are genuinely worthy of trust; a habit of aiming for perfection in executing workouts as you strive to achieve a perfect race; and in applying what you have learned about endurance training, you know execution is never quite as simple as making a plan and following it.

The third pillar is **understanding**, which entails taking a "big picture" approach to prioritizing the various proven training practices; giving more credence to subjective perceptions over objective metrics in assessing how things are going; keeping one eye on short-term fitness building and the other on long-term athletic development; accelerating progress by simplifying your training as much as possible; and using an experimental approach to discover your own optimal training formula.

The fourth pillar is **individuation**, requiring that you become an active partner in decision-making, developing the self-efficacy required to attain mastery; selectively try new things in training to forestall and disrupt complacency; put the most helpful spin possible on the challenges you face through cognitive reframing; shape your training in accordance with your personality and preferences to make it more effective; and operate as a creative problem solver rather than a rote applier of fixed rules.

The fifth pillar is **challenge**, asking that you overcome the natural human tendency toward self-deception, which is essential to mastery; consider restraint at least as important as grit with respect to fulfillment of your potential; approach your sport as a vehicle for becoming the best version of yourself; find the real limit of your ability by continually raising the stakes; and embrace constraints—including the constraint of aging—as opportunities to improve.

Your pursuit of endurance mastery will be unique, but there's no need for you to walk it alone. Remember, self-regulating doesn't mean rejecting any and all help. On the contrary, skillful self-regulation is partly a matter of knowing when you need help, where to get it, and how to use it. I've accompanied you this far, and I and my coaching colleagues are prepared to help you cultivate your full potential in the miles ahead.

That email address again is matt@dreamruncamp.com.

ABOUT THE AUTHOR

Matt Fitzgerald is an acclaimed endurance sports author, coach, and nutritionist. His many books include *Pain & Performance, The Comeback Quotient,* and *80/20 Running.* Matt has also written for a number of leading sports and fitness publications, including *Runner's World* and *Triathlete,* and for popular websites such as outsideonline.com and nbcnews.com.

Matt is cofounder of 80/20 Endurance, the world's premier endurance sports training brand, where athletes can access training plans, videos, and other invaluable resources and inspiration, including a regular 80/20 Endurance podcast and blog. He also codirects the Coaches of Color Initiative, a nonprofit program that seeks to improve diversity in endurance coaching.

A lifelong endurance athlete, Matt speaks frequently at events throughout the United States and internationally and hosts Dream Run Camp, a pro-style residential training camp for runners of all abilities based in Flagstaff, Arizona.